W9-ATD-916

PASTA

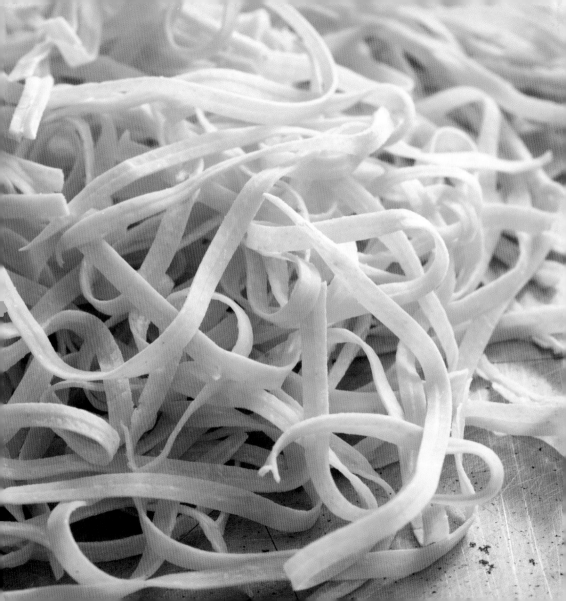

PASTA

carlo middione

PHOTOGRAPHY BY ED ANDERSON

TEN SPEED PRESS
Berkeley | Toronto

Copyright © 2008, 1996, 1982 by Carlo Middione
Photography © 2008 by Ed Anderson

All rights reserved. No part of this book may be reproduced in any form, except brief excerpts for the purpose of review, without written permission of the publisher.

Ten Speed Press
PO Box 7123
Berkeley, California 94707
www.tenspeed.com

Distributed in Australia by Simon and Schuster Australia, in Canada by Ten Speed Press Canada, in New Zealand by Southern Publishers Group, in South Africa by Real Books, and in the United Kingdom and Europe by Publishers Group UK.

Cover and text design by Toni Tajima
Food and prop styling by Jenny Martin-Wong

Previously published as *Carlo Middione's Traditional Pasta* (Ten Speed Press, 1996; 0-89815-805-2) and *Pasta! Cooking It, Loving It* (Chalmers Cookbooks, 1982; 0941034127)

Library of Congress Cataloging-in-Publication Data
Middione, Carlo.
Pasta / Carlo Middione ; photography by
    Ed Anderson.
        p. cm.
Rev. ed.: of Carlo Middione's traditional pasta,
    1996.
Summary: "A collection of fifty authentic pasta
    recipes, including sauce recipes and instruc-
    tions for making pasta from scratch"—
    Provided by publisher.
Includes index.
ISBN-13: 978-1-58008-900-5
ISBN-10: 1-58008-900-3
1. Cookery (Pasta) I. Middione, Carlo. Carlo
    Middione's traditional pasta. II. Title.
TX809.M17M5297 2008
641.8'22—dc22

                  2007039775

Printed in Singapore
First printing, 2008

1 2 3 4 5 6 7 8 9 10 — 12 11 10 09 08

CONTENTS

PREFACE

THIS BOOK HAS HAD so many helpers and dreamers over the years that it is no longer possible to address everyone, but to you all—I love you very much. And in particular, I love my stalwart companion and wife of more than forty years, Lisa Middione, who is, and has been, my muse. Thank you for everything.

I first wrote this book twenty-five years ago, and through several editions, it has remained a mainstay in my own kitchen and in the kitchens and libraries of tens of thousands of people. It still rings true, and this latest edition has been revised, refined, and given a new, contemporary look for today's world. I am pleased and proud that this discourse on pasta has lasted so many years. There is no question these pages have given wisdom, knowledge, direction, and courage to would-be pasta experts and have helped mold them into the real thing. I still get letters telling me so. Many of the dishes herein are on my daily menu at my restaurant, Vivande, in San Francisco.

Of late, there are loads of different Italian dried pastas to choose from, more and better wines than one can imagine from the fertile soils of Italy, and an avalanche of cheeses of every type, so pasta has taken on a new and much broader place in the pantry and at the table. Since the last edition, specialty equipment and ingredients for making pasta are now much more readily available at well-stocked cookware stores and supermarkets and online. Another welcome change is that more and more people realize the importance of pasta as a first dish or main dish in the meal. And many Americans have come to realize that pasta has unique merits that make it delicious on its own.

For many Americans pasta has become a staple, a "must-have" food. Some people eat it because of implied health benefits, some because it is inexpensive, some because they simply cannot live without its tasty, earthy flavor and, if correctly cooked, its texture. The increase in the consumption of pasta has led to a heightened interest in sauces and methods of using pasta in meals. Because of pasta's incredible versatility, one can see that there are endless ways to savor it as a major element in the daily diet.

Me, I *never* tire of pasta. I have tired of eating chocolate bars, meat, and fish, but I say proudly and truthfully I have never tired of pasta, whether I eat it or cook it or serve it. It is my hope that this book will continue to stir up interest in the fun of making and eating pasta so that thousands more will cherish its rewards.

INTRODUCTION

PASTA IS NOT SIMPLY flour and water or eggs. It is a way of life. Pasta knows no social, political, or economic barriers or influences. It is a godsend for the poor, and the richest of the rich have enjoyed pasta with equal gusto. Pasta may well be the most democratic food in the world because it does the most good for the most people.

Medical studies have reported a lower incidence of heart disease and cancer among those who eat pasta daily as long as it is cooked al dente (literally, "to the teeth," or chewy), that is, firm, yet tender. If pasta is cooked thus, it acts like a complex carbohydrate, making it a healthy and thankfully delicious food. (Nutritionists stress the importance of complex carbohydrates, especially in unrefined forms, as focal elements in a healthful diet because they give muscle tissue plenty of food to grow on and far less fat to worry about.)

Personally, I would almost always rather eat a normal serving of good pasta than a steak. I get more immediate satisfaction from the pasta, along with fewer calories and more peace of mind and stomach, than I could possibly get from the meat, although I do enjoy eating meat. Whether made from the whole grain, or refined and enriched with fortified vitamins, the wheat flour in pasta provides a good distribution of essential amino acids to help supply protein, B vitamins (thiamine, riboflavin, and niacin), and iron. The food values are even greater in fresh egg pasta, which is considered to be one of the world's most perfect foods because it contains virtually all of the essential nutrients. Pasta is low in fat and sodium and, if properly prepared and served, easily digested. It is an extraordinarily economical source of excellent nutrition, which can be appropriately dressed up or dressed down for almost any eating occasion.

In tracing the origins of pasta there are, of course, a few givens. We know that our primitive ancestors first gathered wild wheat, discovered how to hull and cook the grain, and learned to mix it with water to make an edible paste. This grain paste was a staple of most prehistoric civilizations, and it has remained a staple in some form ever since.

Relics from the Etruscan civilization of the fourth century B.C. show that these people had developed the tools to mix flour into dough, roll it out on a table, and cut it into strips. The Latin word *nodellus*, meaning the little knot that pasta can get into if you're not careful to be sure the dough isn't sticky, gave us the word "noodles." Other civilizations arrived at the same result using buckwheat, rice, soybeans, mung beans, and other grains and flours.

However, over the centuries, the role of wheat pasta as a significant culinary medium has realized its highest potential in Italy. Nowhere else does pasta show up in so many guises or become such a mainstay and dietary staple as among contemporary Italians, and nowhere else has it achieved cultural expression as an indigenous form of art. There, the pristine and basic flavors of northern Italian *pastasciutta* (any pasta served with sauce) simply dressed with butter and cheese, are at one end of the scale (and the country), while the complex flavors of the delicious and earthy *pasta al forno* (baked pasta) of Sicily in the south represent the other extreme in a very broad range of applications. The pasta dish can take a primary or a secondary place in an Italian meal. Pasta can be very kind to you as a cook when you want to make a particular dish, or you can just see what you have on hand, and pasta will say, "Let's get with it!"

The history of Italian pasta goes back further than most people realize. It certainly predates Marco Polo by a long shot. There is evidence that the Etruscans, who preceded the Romans, already had pasta pretty much as we know it. Farther south, Arabs occupied Sicily for nearly four hundred years. In the twelfth century, they described a concoction called *itriya*, from their word meaning "string," which we know as pasta and was the same as it is made today. Spaghetti in Italian means "little strings." You can see the connection. All over Sicily, pasta became known as *tria*. In Sicily even now, some old-timers still call spaghetti *trii*.

From these tenuous origins, Italians learned to make many pastas by hand, but mostly strings, tubes, and ribbons. Eventually, pasta became a huge industry, feeding masses of Italians since the mid-nineteenth century. Now, Italian pasta exportation is worldwide, and the consumption of pasta continues to grow: per capita consumption in Italy ranges close to 65 pounds per year. America is slowly creeping up in numbers, so let's do our part and join those canny Italians!

That said, Americans must learn to eat their pasta in the approved Italian manner. If you ask for a spoon for your pasta when eating in Italy, you will be taken as uninformed—perhaps a tourist. The way to do it is easy: Use a fork in your right hand only. (You may use it in your left hand, as a concession, if that is natural for you.) Point it downward and twirl it in the pasta until a reasonable amount is entwined on the fork. Now, lift the fork to your mouth and gently but firmly slurp up the ends of the pasta hanging from it.

In Italy's Spaghetti Historical Museum, at Pontedassio, near Genoa, none less than Sophia Loren's advice on spaghetti-eating etiquette is posted thus: "Spaghetti can be eaten successfully if you inhale it like a vacuum cleaner."

MAKING AND COOKING PASTA

"A dish of pasta is only as good as the pasta itself."
—LUIGI BARZINI, author of *The Italians*

THROUGH PASTA'S LONG HISTORY, Italian pasta-makers discovered that hard durum winter wheat flour, rich in gluten, is stronger and superior to ordinary flour for making pasta. They learned that dough made with this flour does not fall apart in boiling water, and is sturdy enough to hold up when formed into a variety of fanciful shapes. Durum wheat is a rich golden yellow with an almost nutlike flavor and a natural spicy fragrance that is sometimes likened to cinnamon. Durum wheat is then milled into *semola* or flour from which the pasta is made. Semolina (*semolino*, in Italian) is merely a coarser, more granular form of this durum flour, which consists almost entirely of the nutritious endosperm particles of the grain.

My standard recipe at my restaurant, Vivande, is 50 percent semolina and 50 percent fancy durum flour (the kind so finely ground it resembles face powder). For 1 pound of mixed flours I use about 4 eggs, but the ratio varies enormously according to the weather, the moisture in the wheat, the moisture in the eggs and their yield, and of course the hand that makes the pasta. This combination of flours makes excellent pasta when using a machine, even a small tabletop, manual roller type. To mix and roll such a pasta totally by hand would be a taxing job, indeed.

Handmade or partially handmade fresh *pasta casalinga* (homemade pasta) is still used widely in Italy. Despite the high quality of Italian commercial dried pasta today and its everyday convenience, there are many who still believe that eating *pasta fresca, fatt' a mano* (fresh pasta, made by hand) is the only way to enjoy the true pasta experience. For sure, both dried and fresh pastas have their place in the pasta diet, as we shall see later in looking at the recipes.

Here is the basic pasta formula I use for good results in the United States:

1 pound all-purpose flour and 4 large U.S. grade A eggs, which yields 1¹/₂ pounds of fresh pasta

Alternatively, the following formula works very well.

BASIC FRESH PASTA DOUGH FORMULA

This recipe yields about 5 or 6 ounces of fresh pasta, which is enough to feed 1 person a generous main-dish serving and possibly 2 to 3 persons a first-course pasta. While 2 ounces of commercial dried pasta are used for a first-course serving per person, remember that fresh pasta is wetter and heavier than the dried.

³/₄ cup unbleached all-purpose flour

1 large egg, at room temperature

In the restaurant kitchen, we describe a batch of pasta by the number of eggs in it; that is, we make a 1-egg pasta, a 2-egg pasta, a 3-egg pasta, and so on by simply increasing the flour proportionately. You can multiply the formula quite easily using the same proportions.

Use an unbleached all-purpose flour for a well-balanced blend of hard and soft wheat flours. Unbleached flour is generally higher in protein and fresher than bleached flour.

Because flour varies with the humidity in the climate, the altitude, and other factors, and because eggs vary in size and in the way the hens that lay them have been fed, this proportion of flour to egg is only approximate and subject to adjustment when you have gained a feel for the optimal consistency of the dough. It should be smooth and supple and hold together without tearing or splitting.

MAKING THE DOUGH

Making pasta by hand is an art, not a science. You must make a lot of it all the time and practice constantly or you will have inconsistency in your results. It is like playing the piano or the violin or, as I have been told, sex. If you don't use it, you lose it.

By Hand

Heap the flour on a wooden or other cool surface and make a well in the center. Add the egg and immediately start to "scramble" the egg into the flour in a circular motion with a fork. Keep pushing bits of flour into the egg. When the mixture holds together well and looks as if you can work it with your hands, do so. Knead the mass for about 6 to 7 minutes to incorporate as much flour as possible. It will be very stiff and hard to work, but do it anyway. (As you work, rest your hands frequently if they become fatigued.) The kneading process is essential to good pasta dough, as it develops the natural elasticity of the flour's gluten, which is a complex combination of proteins.

When properly kneaded, the dough will look satiny. Shape it into a ball, wrap it well in plastic wrap or waxed paper, and let it rest for 20 to 30 minutes at room temperature. Do not refrigerate!

By Food Processor

Place the flour in the work bowl of a food processor fitted with the metal blade. With the machine running, drop in the egg. Process until the mixture resembles grains of sand. Stop the machine and squeeze some of the mixture between your thumb and fingers. It is ready if it clumps together and begins to resemble a dough. (If the mixture is not moist enough to clump together at this point, you can add beaten egg, 1 teaspoon at a time, or a few drops of water if that is easier, until it adheres, and then proceed.)

Turn out the mixture onto a wooden or other cool lightly floured surface. Press the dough together with your hands and knead until it comes together into a shiny, workable mass, about 2 minutes. Shape it into a ball, wrap it well in plastic wrap or waxed paper, and let it rest for 20 to 30 minutes at room temperature. Do not refrigerate!

By Electric Mixer

Larger quantities of pasta can be made in a stand mixer fitted with the paddle attachment. You can successfully make the dough by adding the eggs to the flour in the work bowl and mixing on low speed until the texture of the mixture resembles small peppercorns, about 5 minutes. This will amalgamate the flour and eggs, but you will still have to knead it by hand (as described in the food processor method) for at least a couple of minutes, dividing the dough into smaller portions if necessary. Shape it into a ball (or balls), wrap it well in plastic wrap or waxed paper, and let it rest for 20 to 30 minutes at room temperature. Do not refrigerate!

ROLLING THE DOUGH

Rolling pasta dough by hand is not only a pleasure, but it also frees you from relying on a machine.

By Hand

Dough to be rolled by hand should be made a bit softer by deleting 1 or 2 tablespoons of flour from the formula or by adding more egg. The maximum batch anybody can roll out by hand is a 3-egg pasta, due to the natural limits of the length of the roller, the size of the working surface, and the strength of the person. Also, hand rolling calls for a *mattarello* (roller), which is a smooth, long wooden cylinder 2 inches in diameter and 30 to 36 inches long that you roll with the palms of your hands. (A high-quality wood dowel from a lumberyard or hardware store will work.) The dough should be rolled on a clean wood surface, preferably birch or pine, that is not finished in any way (no varnish or oil). The texture of the wood helps to grip the pasta and gives it a subtle patina—a lovely character—in the opinion of some people.

Have ready a cotton or linen sheet or tablecloth set lightly on a work surface for air-drying the dough. Or, if necessary, you can dry the dough on a clean and lightly floured wooden work surface.

Dust the surface of the board with flour and place the dough on it. Flatten the ball of dough with your hands into a disk about $1/2$ inch thick. Put the rolling pin across the center of the disk and start to roll it away from you. Maintaining even pressure, repeat rolling outward from the center, rotating the dough by quarters or thirds as you work to keep it round (if it turns out to be oval, don't worry). Don't compress the dough or lean on the *mattarello* while you are rolling so the dough circle remains evenly thick. Just roll and stretch the dough without flattening it down. Continue until the dough is as thin as you can possibly make it without tearing. It should be less than $^1/_{16}$ inch thick. Even though it may seem very thin, remember that it will contract and thicken slightly while drying.

When the dough is the approximate desired thickness, you can thin it even further and prevent it from contracting with this little maneuver, which sounds more difficult than it really is: Place the *mattarello* at the top of the dough sheet. Drape the top edge of the dough sheet over and around the *mattarello* and roll up about a quarter of the dough sheet (like a paper towel). Put your hands on the dough in the center of the *mattarello* and very quickly roll it back and forth about 3 to 4 inches each way. As you roll, press down firmly with your hands and move them apart, out across the dough, until they reach the opposite ends of the roller. Drape over another quarter of the dough (bringing you to the halfway mark on the dough circle) and repeat the process. Then, unfurl the dough sheet, turn it around, and do the same steps from the other end. Repeat the full process twice. The dough is now ready for drying, prior to being cut into shapes.

Put the sheet of pasta on a large cotton or linen sheet or tablecloth, or on your cleaned and floured board. Let it air-dry for about 10 minutes on one side. Then carefully roll it up on the *mattarello* to facilitate handling. Unroll it and expose the other side to the air, and let dry for a bit. The total drying time should be about 15 minutes. The dough should feel like a piece of fine-quality chamois leather—soft and supple, but strong and not sticky in any way. Drying time will vary, depending on the humidity of the air and the temperature of the room. This is only a guide. Your experience will lead you to produce better and better pasta every time you make it.

PASTA MACHINE MAINTENANCE

Properly used and cleaned, your manual pasta-rolling machine will last a lifetime in perfect condition. To get the most out of yours, please observe the following guidelines:

- Always secure a hand-crank machine to a heavy table or countertop for maximum stability before using. An electronic machine should be heavy and have stabilizing feet.
- Always separate the dough into workable portions. Never overload the machine, or it will bind or break the dough—and start to break up its own mechanism. *Never* put stress on the machine. It will do all that you want it to do, but don't abuse it. If necessary, remove the piece of dough and make it a little smaller.
- Always start the dough in the widest open position of the rollers, and turn the crank at moderate speed. *Do not* try to set world records.
- Always lower the roller setting one notch at a time to avoid straining the mechanism.
- Keep your pasta machine scrupulously clean. Use a medium-stiff dry brush to clean the rollers and all the corners and exposed parts. Brush everything thoroughly with the dry brush and use it *only* for this purpose. Then wipe the machine down with a dry cloth. Never, *ever* put any water on the machine, not even from a damp cloth, or you will destroy it in short order. Store the machine in its box in a clean location between uses.

By Manual or Electric Pasta Rollers

After the dough has rested for about 20 minutes, cut it into thirds, unless you are using the *mattarello* to roll out the entire batch of dough. Flatten one-third into a disk or rectangle about ¼ inch thick. Tightly cover the remaining dough with plastic wrap to keep it from drying out while you work with the first portion.

Have ready a cotton or linen sheet or tablecloth set on a work surface for air-drying the rolled pasta. Or, if necessary, you can dry the pasta on a clean and lightly floured wooden work surface.

Feed the dough through the widest opening of the smooth rollers. Then fold it in thirds like a letter and feed it through twice more; for each pass, decrease the space between the rollers a notch and flour the pasta as much as necessary to keep it from sticking. When it is very thin (use your judgment as to how thin it should be, but try for ¹/₃₂ inch thick. Dry as described in the preceding section on rolling the dough by hand.

COLORED PASTAS

At the risk of being branded a heretic, I must tell you that I consider colored pastas, at best, a gimmick. Only occasionally have I encountered colored pasta in Italy in public eating places. In my opinion, it is aesthetically and gastronomically unnecessary to worry about colors in your homemade pasta, with the possible exception of green spinach noodles, which are a nice occasional variation.

If you want to try making colored pasta, you will find it easier to mix the dough with a food processor than by hand. Take about ½ cup of cooked spinach, tomato, or whatever vegetable whose color you want to give the pasta and squeeze it as dry as you can in paper towels. (This is easier if you have steamed the vegetable in as little water as possible.) For example, beets have a bright color. You can also dry it by tossing in a dry frying pan, or by blowing it with a hair dryer; better yet, cook it the day before and let it air-dry overnight. Puree the vegetable in a food processor; add the flour and process well before adding the egg (as a guide to the amount of egg the mixture will take). You may have to reduce the amount of egg lest the dough become too soft.

Once you've made the colored dough, proceed exactly as for plain.

Incidentally, my remarks about colored pasta do not apply to the natural whole-wheat pasta used a lot in and around Venice. To make this, try replacing up to 70 percent of the unbleached all-purpose flour in your formula with whole-wheat flour, and proceed as usual. You will have to develop the right amounts on an ad hoc basis, incorporating as much whole wheat as the pasta will take.

CUTTING THE PASTA

To hand-cut long pasta shapes, roll out a 12-inch-long lightly floured sheet of pasta. Using a very sharp knife, cut to the desired width ($^1/_4$ inch for fettuccine, $^1/_{16}$ inch for tagliolini, $^1/_2$ to $^3/_4$ inch for pappardelle, and so on). Gently unroll the cuts and lightly dust with flour.

To cut long pasta with a machine, hand-cut a sheet of pasta no more than 12 inches long and as wide as your machine allows. Attach the appropriate cutting attachment to your machine. Start slowly and roll the sheet through until it is completely cut. Gently fluff the pasta immediately to keep it from sticking or clumping. If necessary, you may also want to sprinkle it with flour.

Extruding pasta machines have different methods. Follow the manufacturer's instructions.

COOKING PASTA

Boil, boil, toil, and trouble! The first two words apply where pasta is concerned. The latter two are inaccurate if you follow some simple rules that will get you through the cooking of pasta without the toil or trouble. Keep in mind that pasta to be served with a sauce should be eaten immediately after cooking. The sauce should be ready and waiting. The bowls or plates should be heated. Toss the pasta in some of the sauce (use a separate heated serving bowl or the empty pot in which it was cooked), serve it, and pass additional sauce and cheese, as the recipe directs.

Pasta that will be baked—as for lasagne—must be undercooked in the initial boiling as it will continue to cook as it bakes in the sauce. To cool the pasta and quickly stop it from cooking further when it has reached the desired level of doneness, immediately plunge it into cold water—the only situation where you would need to stop the cooking in this way. Also, undercook pasta if it will be stuffed and baked, when preparing cannelloni or pasta shells, for example. Otherwise it will overcook and become soggy.

Stuffed pastas, such as tortellini, ravioli, and pansotti, are cooked the same way as plain pasta—in other words, in boiling, salted water. Since they are made with fresh pasta, they will cook faster than packaged dried pasta, usually 5 minutes should do it. Test at 4 minutes and you will be able to judge the timing better. If the stuffed pastas are frozen, proceed as directed, but add 1 minute to the cooking time. I like to scoop stuffed pastas out of the cooking water with a big slotted spoon. This keeps them from falling apart.

To cook pasta, use a large pot that can hold lots of water so the pasta can float freely while cooking. One that heats quickly is a boon as you should allow at least 4 to 5 quarts of water per pound of pasta—that's a lot of liquid to bring to a boil. Too little water prevents the pasta from cooking evenly, and the pieces may stick together as a result.

Bring the water to a galloping boil. When the water is boiling briskly, add salt, preferably not iodized, 1$^1/_2$ teaspoons for every quart of water. (If the salt is added before the water boils, it may leave a residual taste of phenol on delicate pastas.) *Never* add oil to the pasta-cooking water to prevent sticking. It makes the sauce slide off. If you follow these directions, you shouldn't have any problems with sticking.

Drop the pasta into the boiling, salted water. Long pastas should be in manageable lengths. Commercial dried pastas, especially, will expand during cooking. To get very long pastas into the pot, grasp a bundle of them at one end and plunge the other end into the boiling water; as the submerged pasta softens, gradually let the bundle slide into the pot of boiling water without breaking. Stir well to prevent sticking.

As the pasta cooks, watch it carefully. Homemade fresh egg pasta will cook in seconds or minutes. Commercial dried pastas generally cook in 7 to 8 minutes, depending on size. Cappellini are so thin they cook al dente in 50 seconds. When first drained they look spiky, but when sauced and tossed they quickly become supple and easy to eat. You can be guided to some extent by the directions on the package, but it is still essential to watch the pasta very closely as it cooks and to test it frequently for doneness. Pasta is done when it tests al dente (to the tooth), is tender but very firm, still bitable and not mushy, with no taste of flour. Immediately remove it from the boiling water with a pasta rake or a slotted spoon, or it can be drained in a colander. Be sure the pasta remains nicely wet, or it will absorb too much sauce and probably stick together.

USING AND SERVING PASTA

Italians have raised the making and eating of pasta to a fine art. Here are just a few tips to keep in mind:

- The taste of pasta varies with the thickness and texture of the particular cut.
- Fresh pasta, which (especially when rolled) is distinctly firm and springy yet deliciously tender, will absorb sauces more readily than commercial dried pasta.
- The delicacy of fresh pasta deserves the lightest, least assertive saucing.
- Delicate sauces are best served with delicate pasta.
- Tubular and concave pasta shapes like rigatoncini and chiocciole are designed to trap sauces. Use them when you want to eat a lot of sauce in each bite.
- Serve a rich sauce, such as carbonara, with a flat ribbon pasta or a shape like spaghetti or fettuccine, which will not trap or accumulate too much of the sauce in each bite.
- While one school of thought holds that you should drink water with pasta and no wine until afterward, the majority of Italians enjoy wine with their pasta.
- The wines to accompany pasta are chosen to go well with the particular sauce used. In Italy, a wine of the same region as the pasta dish is generally served, but I like to be adventurous and pair wines and pastas from different regions.

The more deeply you become involved in the experience yourself, the better you will be able to orchestrate the broad range of opportunities pasta offers to satisfy your own taste and enjoyment of eating.

BASIC
SAUCES

salse di base

SALSA DI POMODORO STRACOTTO

SLOW TOMATO SAUCE makes 10 cups

This is the classic approach to the richer, heavier, and traditionally darker-colored tomato sauce, which is cooked slowly for a long time. If good fresh tomatoes are available to you, use the same weight as that given for the canned tomatoes in the recipe and prepare as directed in Quick Tomato Sauce (page 19). I like this sauce best on baked pasta or on big, stubby boiled pasta like rigatoni.

¼ cup extra virgin olive oil

1   large yellow onion, finely chopped

3   cloves garlic, finely chopped

2   (28-ounce) cans tomatoes, seeded and coarsely chopped, including juice

1   cup water

1   cup red wine

¼ cup tomato paste

1   sprig fresh oregano, or 1 teaspoon dried

Sea salt and freshly ground black pepper

Place the oil and onion in a large, heavy saucepan over medium-high heat. Sauté until the onion is soft and translucent, about 5 minutes. Add the garlic and sauté until golden, 2 minutes more. Add the tomatoes, water, wine, tomato paste, and oregano; season with salt and pepper. Decrease the heat to low and simmer, uncovered, for 3 hours, stirring occasionally.

Serve immediately over pasta or transfer to a jar. Let cool, then cover the jar tightly and store in the refrigerator for up to 5 days or in the freezer for up to 6 weeks.

SALSA AL POMODORO QUICK TOMATO SAUCE

makes a generous 8 cups

This is a fresh-tasting, almost tart sauce that is excellent for pasta. It is also known as *salsa alla marinara* (sailor sauce). The same weight of fresh, *ripe* tomatoes may be used. Using the red pepper flakes will produce a more profound taste. The fast cooking will help to reduce the sauce and make it thick, but be careful that it does not burn on the bottom.

NOTE: The same base can be used in making fish stew, by adding $1/3$ cup or more of white or red wine before cooking, and then adding the fish and shellfish just minutes before serving.

$1/2$ cup extra virgin olive oil

1 large yellow onion, finely chopped

2 cloves garlic, finely chopped

2 (28-ounce) cans tomatoes, finely chopped, including juice

1 sprig fresh oregano, or $1^1/2$ teaspoons dried

4 leaves fresh basil, or $1^1/2$ teaspoons dried

Pinch of red pepper flakes (optional)

Sea salt and freshly ground black pepper

Place the oil and onion in a large, heavy saucepan over medium-high heat. Sauté until the onion is soft and translucent, about 5 minutes. Add the garlic and sauté about 3 minutes more. Add the tomatoes, oregano, basil, and red pepper flakes; season with salt and pepper. Continue to cook, uncovered, about 15 minutes, stirring occasionally, so the sauce does not burn on the bottom.

Serve immediately over pasta or transfer to a jar. Let cool, then cover the jar tightly and store in the refrigerator for up to 4 days or in the freezer for up to 6 weeks.

PESTO POUNDED HERB SAUCE makes about 1 cup

Traditional pesto from Genoa is delicious alone or as a topping for pasta. It can also be used as a decorative dressing for sliced hard-boiled eggs served as an appetizer, as a sauce for grilled meats or fish, as a sauce for sliced sun-ripened fresh tomatoes, in salads, in omelets, and in whichever other ways an adventurous taste exploration would elect. The sauce was originally made by hand with a mortar and pestle, but a food processor does an adequate job.

1 cup tightly packed fresh basil leaves

1 large clove garlic

1 heaping tablespoon freshly grated Parmesan cheese

1 tablespoon freshly grated Romano cheese

1 teaspoon pine nuts or walnuts

2/3 cup extra virgin olive oil (adjust less or more, depending on the desired thickness of pesto)

Sea salt and freshly ground black pepper

In the work bowl of a food processor fitted with the metal blade, add the basil, garlic, Parmesan and Romano cheeses, and pine nuts. Pulse until all is finely chopped. With the machine running, gradually add the oil, processing constantly until the sauce has reached the desired consistency, like loose mayonnaise; season with salt and pepper.

Serve immediately over pasta or transfer to a jar and cover with olive oil. Cover the jar tightly and store in the refrigerator for up to 2 weeks or the freezer for up to 6 weeks.

SALSA BOLOGNESE (OR RAGÙ)

BOLOGNESE MEAT SAUCE makes about 2¹/₂ cups

In America, this is the most popular and best known of the famous Italian ragù (literally, "stew") meat sauces. While purists know that a ragù starts with a solid piece of meat, hand-cut with a knife or even snipped with kitchen scissors into tiny morsels, ground meat is used here for convenience.

2 ounces prosciutto di Parma fat or pancetta, finely chopped (about ¹/₄ cup)

1 yellow onion, finely chopped

1 carrot, finely chopped

1 tender, inner yellow stalk celery, including leaves, finely chopped

12 ounces ground beef round

¹/₂ clove garlic, halved again

1 cup red wine

¹/₂ cup heavy cream

1 teaspoon sea salt

¹/₄ teaspoon freshly ground black pepper

1 cup finely chopped fresh or canned tomatoes, including juice

Put the prosciutto fat in a large, heavy saucepan and sauté over medium heat until it melts. Add the onion, carrot, and celery and sauté, stirring occasionally, until the mixture becomes a light golden color, about 6 minutes; add the meat, breaking it up with a fork, and cook, stirring frequently, until it just loses its pink color. Add the garlic and red wine. Cook until the wine evaporates, about 10 to 15 minutes, stirring occasionally. Add the cream and decrease the heat to low; cook gently until the cream practically disappears, about 10 minutes, then add the salt and pepper. Add the tomatoes and cook gently for about 2 hours, stirring occasionally. The result should be a thick and lovely mass resembling a puree.

Serve immediately over pasta or transfer to a jar. Let cool, then cover the jar tightly and store in the refrigerator for up to 5 days or in the freezer for up to 6 weeks.

BALSAMELLA BÉCHAMEL OR WHITE SAUCE

makes 2 cups

This is a simple and reliable basic white sauce, widely useful in general cooking as well as with pasta. Known as béchamel in French cooking, the sauce actually originated as balsamella or besciamella in Italy long before the sixteenth century, when Catherine de' Medici brought it to France. An Italian fourteenth-century manuscript of the recipe is as valid today as it was then.

NOTE: If you do not wish to use this sauce right away, butter a piece of parchment or waxed paper and push the buttered side right down against the surface of the sauce, pressing the paper tightly against the sides of the pan to keep all the air off the surface. You can also thin or thicken the sauce by simply adding more or less of the liquid and solid ingredients.

2   cups whole milk

1   grating fresh nutmeg (optional)

1   slice onion (optional)

1   clove garlic (optional)

1   bay leaf (optional)

3   tablespoons unsalted butter

3   tablespoons unbleached all-purpose flour

Sea salt and ground white pepper

Heat the milk in a heavy saucepan over low heat (do not let it boil) and infuse it with any or all of the optional flavorings by simply dropping them in the milk. Keep it hot.

In another heavy saucepan, add the butter and cook over medium heat until it is melted and bubbling, about 1 minute. Add the flour all at once, stirring constantly with a whisk. Let the mixture cook for about 2 minutes. Take it off the heat for a moment and then add the hot milk, straining the milk through a small sieve into the pan. Season with salt and white pepper. Put the sauce back on the heat. Cook and stir constantly until it begins to boil, about 5 minutes. Then decrease the heat to medium-low and cook, stirring, until the mixture is thick and glossy. Use it immediately. To store, let cool completely, cover tightly, and refrigerate for up to 4 days.

PASTA WITH SAUCE

pastasciutta

SPAGHETTI AGLIO E OLIO

SPAGHETTI WITH GARLIC AND OLIVE OIL serves 4 to 6

This is a famous, simple pasta which many Italians call their favorite. Some say they eat it when they feel sad because it makes them feel happy again. Well, garlic *is* supposed to have curative powers. SUGGESTED WINES: BARBARESCO OR LACRYMA CHRISTI DEL VESUVIO

½ cup extra virgin olive oil

4 large cloves garlic, finely chopped

12 ounces dried spaghetti

½ cup finely chopped fresh Italian parsley

Pinch of red pepper flakes (optional)

Freshly ground or cracked black pepper

Place the oil and garlic in a heavy skillet over medium heat and sauté until the garlic is light golden in color, about 1 minute. Remove from the heat and set aside.

Have a heated serving bowl ready. Cook the spaghetti al dente (see page 13), and drain well. Transfer the pasta to the serving bowl.

Add the parsley to the oil and garlic in the skillet and mix together. Work quickly. Pour the mixture on the cooked pasta, add the pepper flakes, and mix well. Sprinkle with black pepper and serve very hot. No cheese on this dish, please!

VARIATION: To make Spaghetti alla Carrettiere (Spaghetti Carter-Style), which is equally good and popular, make as directed above and add grated Pecorino Romano or Sardo cheese when serving it.

FETTUCCINE AL BURRO
THIN RIBBON PASTA WITH BUTTER serves 4 to 6

This is the very simple way many northern Italians prefer to enjoy their pasta. Butter is king in the north, while extra virgin olive oil is king in the south.

SUGGESTED WINES: ALCAMO BIANCO OR SOAVE

³/₄ cup unsalted butter

1   pound fresh fettuccine, or 12 ounces dried

¹/₂ cup freshly grated Parmesan cheese, plus additional for passing

Freshly ground black pepper, for sprinkling

Place the butter in a warm serving dish and allow it to become very soft and supple, but not separated.

Cook the fettuccine al dente (see page 13), and drain well. Immediately transfer the cooked pasta to the dish of butter, and toss gently. Add the cheese and toss gently again. Grind on the pepper. Serve at once, while hot! Pass the additional cheese at the table.

VARIATION: To make Fettuccine al Burro e Pinoli, follow the directions above, but add 5 tablespoons toasted pine nuts as follows: To brown the nuts, cook them in a heavy skillet over low heat, using no butter or oil, stirring continuously. When they are golden in color, about 5 minutes, immediately transfer them from the pan to a cool plate, and set aside. Add the pine nuts at the final tossing and serve the pasta immediately.

CHIOCCIOLE AL MASCARPONE E NOCI
SMALL PASTA WITH MASCARPONE AND WALNUTS

serves 6

This elegant first-course pasta should be eaten in small amounts. It is one of the many wonderful Italian pasta dishes that are still relatively unfamiliar in America.

SUGGESTED WINES: ALCAMO BIANCO OR MONTEPULCIANO D'ABRUZZO

1½ tablespoons unsalted butter

8 ounces mascarpone cheese

12 ounces dried 1-inch shell pasta

3 tablespoons freshly grated Parmesan cheese, plus additional for passing

2 to 3 ounces walnut meats, coarsely chopped, plus additional larger pieces for garnish

Melt the butter over low heat in a heatproof serving dish. Add the mascarpone and melt it slowly, stirring now and then. *Do not let it boil.*

Cook the pasta al dente (see page 13). Drain it, leaving a few spoonfuls of water coating the shells. Add the pasta to the mascarpone-butter mixture and stir it all around. Add the Parmesan and the chopped walnuts and mix again. Serve hot, garnished with the larger walnut pieces, and pass the additional Parmesan at the table.

SPAGHETTI CON LE COZZE
SPAGHETTI WITH MUSSELS serves 6

Try to use mussels harvested from icy cold waters, that are not too big, and that smell like an ocean breeze. SUGGESTED WINES: CHARDONNAY OR PINOT BIANCO

3 pounds mussels

1/4 cup extra virgin olive oil

3 cloves garlic, finely chopped

Sea salt and freshly ground black pepper

1 cup dry white wine

1 cup Salsa al Pomodoro (Quick Tomato Sauce, page 19)

8 ounces dried spaghetti or 14 ounces fresh fettuccine

1/3 cup chopped fresh Italian parsley

Scrub the mussels with a vegetable brush, and pull off any "beard" they may have. Soak them in very cold water for about 30 minutes, shaking often; drain well.

Put the oil in a very large, heavy skillet over medium-low heat; add the garlic, some salt and pepper, and the mussels. Shake the pan vigorously, and add the wine. Increase the heat to medium-high, add the tomato sauce, and boil for a moment. The mussels should open in about 2 minutes. Do not overcook.

Cook the pasta al dente (see page 13) and drain, leaving in a bit of cooking water on the pasta. (If using dried pasta, start cooking it *before* you cook the mussels.)

Quickly remove the mussels from the pan with tongs and arrange them around the rim of individual serving plates. Discard any mussels that do not open.

Add the pasta to the sauce and stir well. Place the pasta in the center of each plate, sprinkle heavily with the parsley, and serve immediately. Please, no cheese.

PENNE AL SALMONE
"PEN" MACARONI WITH SMOKED SALMON serves 6

If you're fond of smoked salmon, this unusual pasta recipe makes a delightful first course or nice brunch dish. Since the smoked salmon is chopped for the sauce, you may be able to economize by buying scraps or trimmings, less expensive than whole slices. SUGGESTED WINES: ORVIETO OR PINOT GRIGIO

3   tablespoons unsalted butter

1   cup heavy cream

3   ounces best-cure smoked salmon (mildly salted and smoked), finely chopped

1   tablespoon finely chopped shallot

Juice of ½ large lemon

2   ounces Scotch whisky

Sea salt and ground white pepper

12 ounces dried penne

Freshly ground black pepper, for sprinkling

Melt the butter in a large, heavy skillet over low heat; add the cream and reduce by one-third, about 5 minutes. Add the salmon and shallot and cook for about 2 minutes. Add the lemon juice and mix well. Add the whisky and cook long enough to let the alcohol evaporate, about 1 minute. Season with salt and white pepper. Mix well. Keep the salmon warm while the pasta cooks.

Cook the penne very al dente (see page 13), and drain well. Add the well-drained pasta to the salmon mixture in the skillet and mix gently to thoroughly coat and finish cooking the pasta. If the sauce is too dry, add some more cream. It should be very smooth and creamy, but the pasta should not swim in it. Serve hot. Freshly ground black pepper atop each serving finishes this dish.

TRENETTE AL PESTO PASTA WITH PESTO SAUCE

serves 6

This is always a favorite. The beautiful green color, heady aroma, and exquisite flavor of the pesto add up to a real taste treat. Followed by a breaded veal cutlet, a green salad, and some fresh fruit with cheese, this can be a memorable meal.

SUGGESTED WINES: BARBARESCO OR CHIANTI RISERVA

1 pound fresh trenette pasta, or 12 ounces dried

1/4 cup extra virgin olive oil

1 cup Pesto (Pounded Herb Sauce, page 20), at room temperature

Sea salt and freshly ground black pepper

1/2 cup freshly grated Parmesan cheese, for passing

Have a heated serving bowl ready. Cook the pasta al dente (see page 13). Drain, but reserve about 3/4 cup of the pasta water. Place the pasta in the serving bowl. Add the oil and toss well. Dilute the sauce with some of the pasta water until it is just loose but not runny; add the diluted sauce to the bowl, and toss with the pasta. Season with salt and pepper and serve. Pass the cheese at the table.

PASTA ERICINA PASTA AS MADE IN ERICE, SICILY

serves 3 to 4

The ancient and picturesque town Erice is perched on top of a mountain high above the city of Trapani on the southwest coast of Sicily. Fresh Erice sauce is used at room temperature, but it can be very gently heated and served on hot or cold green beans or as a condiment for salmon or chicken. It should not be boiled or cooked at all. SUGGESTED WINES: CIRÒ ROSATO OR CORVO ROSSO

1½ pounds fresh tomatoes, cored and peeled, or 1 (28-ounce) can tomatoes, including juice

3 tablespoons extra virgin olive oil

6 leaves fresh basil, chopped, or 1 teaspoon dried

Sea salt and freshly ground black pepper

10 ounces fresh fettuccine or 8 ounces dried spaghetti or penne

½ cup finely chopped fresh Italian parsley

2 cloves garlic, finely chopped

Chop the tomatoes finely, transfer them to a mixing bowl with their juice, and add the olive oil and basil; season with salt and pepper. Let the mixture stand at room temperature for at least 1 hour to blend well.

Have a heated serving dish ready. Cook the pasta al dente (see page 13), and drain well. Return it to the cooking pot, add some of the tomato sauce, mix well, and then add the rest. Transfer the pasta to the serving dish and top with the chopped parsley. Sprinkle on the garlic and serve.

PASTA ALL SCIAQUINA

PASTA WASHERWOMAN-STYLE serves 4

This pasta with its humble name is actually quite elegant and fit for a king. Italians have fun with naming their dishes. The cream, prosciutto, and best imported Parmesan combine here to achieve an absolutely irresistible result. Fettuccine, linguine, and penne are also good choices for this dish.

SUGGESTED WINES: CABERNET SAUVIGNON OR CHIANTI RISERVA

2 1/2 cups Salsa al Pomodoro (Quick Tomato Sauce, page 19), pureed

1/2 cup heavy cream

4 ounces prosciutto di Parma, finely chopped

Sea salt and freshly ground black pepper

8 ounces dried spaghetti or other long pasta

1/3 cup finely chopped fresh Italian parsley

Freshly grated Parmesan cheese, for sprinkling

In a heavy saucepan, combine the pureed tomato sauce, the cream, and the prosciutto. Heat gently over medium heat for about 10 minutes. Season with salt and pepper. Keep warm while the pasta cooks.

Have a heated serving dish ready. Cook the pasta al dente (page 13), and drain well. Transfer the pasta to the serving dish. Add some sauce and toss. Add more sauce and then sprinkle on the parsley. Finally, sprinkle the cheese over each portion and serve.

LINGUINE ALLE VONGOLE PASTA WITH CLAMS

serves 4

This is a deservedly popular dish. It is quick and easy to make, at least with canned clams, which are available almost everywhere. It can make a satisfying meal along with a green salad, a piece of fruit, and some good coffee.

SUGGESTED WINES: PINOT BIANCO OR VERDICCHIO

3 pounds small clams in their shells, or 2 (7-ounce) cans chopped clams in their juice

1/3 cup extra virgin olive oil

2 or 3 large cloves garlic, finely chopped

Sea salt and plenty of freshly ground black pepper

Generous pinch of red pepper flakes, or 1/3 cup heavy cream (optional)

2 tablespoons chopped fresh Italian parsley

8 ounces dried linguine, spaghetti, or other long pasta

Wash the clams' shells well, scrubbing them with a brush to remove the sand and debris. Place them in a large, heavy skillet with 1 tablespoon of the oil. Cover the pan and cook on high heat until the shells open wide, about 3 minutes. You may serve the clams in their shells, or remove them and discard the shells at this point. Either way, set them aside. Then, strain the pan juices through a fine sieve to eliminate additional bits of shell and sand. Reserve the liquid. (If using canned clams, strain and reserve the juice and clams, separated.)

Put the rest of the oil and the garlic in a clean skillet over medium heat. Brown the garlic well, but do not burn, about 1 minute. Add the reserved clam juice, salt and pepper, and either the red pepper flakes or the cream. Add the parsley and clams. Remove from the heat; set aside.

continued

Have a heated serving bowl ready. Cook the pasta al dente (see page 13), and drain well. Transfer the pasta to the serving bowl. Pour the hot clam sauce over it (reheat the sauce first, if necessary) and mix well. Serve at once. Please—do not serve this dish with cheese.

PASTA ALLA NORMA
PASTA WITH FRIED EGGPLANT serves 4 to 6

The dish is known variously as *pasta con melanzane* (eggplant), *pasta alla Norma* (the opera), or *pasta alla Bellini* (after the great Sicilian composer who wrote the opera). In Sicily you simply order "Norma"—they know what you want.

SUGGESTED WINES: REGALEALI ROSSO OR CANNONAU DI SARDEGNA

1   large, plump eggplant

$1/2$ cup extra virgin olive oil

Sea salt and freshly ground black pepper

12 ounces dried spaghetti, rigatoni, or penne

4   cups Salsa al Pomodoro (Quick Tomato Sauce, page 19)

Line a dish with paper towels. Slice the eggplant lengthwise into $1/4$-inch-thick slices. Do not remove the skin. (If the eggplant is truly fresh, there is no need to salt and "leach" it, because the juice will not be bitter.) Heat the oil over medium heat in a large, heavy skillet, add the eggplant slices, and fry until nicely browned on both sides, about 2 minutes per side. (Or, to conserve oil, you can liberally brush the eggplant slices with some oil and broil them.) Transfer them

About 20 large leaves fresh basil, chopped medium-fine

½ cup freshly grated ricotta salata or pecorino cheese, for passing

to the prepared dish. Sprinkle with salt and pepper, and set aside.

Have ready a heated serving bowl and individual serving plates. Cook the pasta al dente (see page 13), and drain well. Reheat the sauce, if necessary. Transfer the pasta to the serving bowl. Add a little of the sauce and toss. Serve on the heated plates. Spoon a good amount of sauce on top of each portion and carefully lay 1 or 2 slices of fried eggplant on top of or alongside the sauce. Sprinkle about 1 teaspoon of chopped fresh basil on top of each serving and pass the cheese at the table.

BUCATINI ALL'AMATRICIANA
BUCATINI WITH PANCETTA AND TOMATO serves 6

This dish comes from the town of Amatrice near the east coast of Italy by the Adriatic Sea. It has been adopted by the Romans, however, who have made the dish their own by adding some hot red pepper flakes. SUGGESTED WINES: BARBARESCO OR VINO NOBILE DI MONTEPULCIANO

2   tablespoons extra virgin olive oil

6   ounces pancetta, diced very small or thinly sliced (about a generous 1/2 cup)

1   small yellow onion, finely chopped

5 or 6 small fresh or canned tomatoes, cored, peeled, seeded, and diced

Sea salt and freshly ground black pepper

12 ounces dried bucatini, perciatelle, or penne

Generous pinch of red pepper flakes

1/2 cup freshly grated pecorino cheese, plus additional for passing

Heat the oil in a heavy skillet over medium heat. Add the pancetta and onion and sauté, stirring, until lightly golden in color, about 5 minutes. Add the chopped tomatoes and cook gently, about 5 minutes, but do not let them get too soft. The pieces should remain intact; taste and season with the salt and pepper. Set aside and keep warm.

Have a heated serving bowl ready. Cook the pasta al dente (see page 13), and drain well. Place the pasta in the serving bowl. Add the sauce and toss well. Adjust for salt and pepper, and then add the pepper flakes and the 1/2 cup cheese. Toss once more and serve hot, passing the additional cheese at the table.

MACCHERONI AI QUATTRO FORMAGGI

MACARONI WITH FOUR CHEESES serves 6 .

This is a rich and luxurious pasta, due to the *abbondanza* (abundance) of beautiful cheeses used in the sauce. It makes an important first course for a special occasion menu. Be sure to follow it with a light entrée, such as veal scaloppine, squab, rack of lamb, or game. SUGGESTED WINES: MONTEPULCIANO D'ABRUZZO OR BAROLO

$^{1}/_{2}$ **cup unsalted butter**

$^{1}/_{2}$ **cup heavy cream, at room temperature (or warmer)**

$^{1}/_{3}$ **cup mashed Gorgonzola cheese**

$^{1}/_{3}$ **cup shredded fontina cheese**

$^{1}/_{3}$ **cup shredded Taleggio cheese**

12 **ounces of any dried macaroni, such as rigatoni, penne, chiocciole, or other fancy shape**

Sea salt and freshly ground black pepper

$^{1}/_{2}$ **cup freshly grated Parmesan cheese, for passing**

Heat the butter and cream in a large, heavy saucepan over medium-low heat, being careful to keep it from boiling. Add the Gorgonzola, fontina, and Taleggio cheeses to the cream and butter, whisking gently. Maintain the heat until they melt, keeping the sauce well whisked and blended. Remove from the heat, set aside, and keep warm.

Have a heated serving bowl ready. Cook the pasta al dente (see page 13), and drain well. Transfer the pasta to the serving bowl. Pour over the thick, melted cheese sauce and toss well. Season with salt and pepper.

Serve this dish piping hot. Pass the Parmesan at the table.

FETTUCCINE ALLA ROMANA (FETTUCCINE ALLA PANNA)
RIBBON PASTA WITH CREAM, BUTTER, AND CHEESE
serves 6

This pasta has become popularly known as "Fettuccine Alfredo" after the Alfredo Restaurant in Rome. Alfredo "introduced" this dish to America at the 1939 World's Fair in New York, where he complained that he needed water from the aqueducts in Rome to make the dish really perfect! The measurements given in this recipe are only a guide. SUGGESTED WINES: PINOT BIANCO OR SOAVE

- ³/₄ cup unsalted butter, at room temperature
- 1 pound fresh fettuccine, or 12 ounces dried
- 1¹/₂ cups heavy cream, at warm room temperature
- 1 cup freshly grated Parmesan cheese, plus additional for passing
- 7 or 8 big gratings of fresh nutmeg, or a generous pinch of dried
- Freshly ground black or white pepper

Place the butter in a large, heavy skillet and put it in a warm place, even over very low heat, to melt, but not cook.

Cook the pasta al dente (see page 13), and quickly drain it, leaving it slightly wet. Immediately put the drained pasta into the skillet with the butter and toss all around to coat the pasta well. Add the cream and the 1 cup grated cheese and gently toss again. Add the nutmeg and pepper and serve the pasta, which should be eaten immediately. Pass the additional cheese at the table.

SPAGHETTI ALLA CARBONARA

SPAGHETTI COAL VENDOR-STYLE serves 4 to 6

Some say this is a relatively new pasta recipe, originating in Rome after World War II when the Allied troops restored the city's supplies of eggs and bacon. Others say the dish has been made around the Sicilian coal mines since ancient times. I subscribe to the latter belief. SUGGESTED WINES: AGLIANICO OR MONTEPULCIANO D'ABRUZZO

NOTE: It is imperative that you use only high-quality salmonella-free eggs.

2 tablespoons extra virgin olive oil

4 cloves garlic, slightly crushed

5 to 8 ounces pancetta, sliced 1/8 inch thick and coarsely chopped

Generous 1/4 cup dry white wine

4 large eggs, slightly beaten

Sea salt and a generous amount of freshly ground black pepper

1/2 cup or more freshly grated Romano or Parmesan cheese (or a mix of both), plus additional for passing

12 ounces dried spaghetti

Put the oil and garlic in a heavy skillet and cook over medium heat until the garlic is golden, about 1 minute. Discard the garlic. Add the pancetta to the pan and cook, stirring, until it is a light golden color, 2 to 3 minutes. Do not let it burn. Add the wine and let the mixture simmer for 3 or 4 minutes. Remove the pan from the heat and set aside.

In the bowl from which you will serve the pasta, place the beaten eggs, salt and pepper, and the 1/2 cup cheese. Mix the ingredients with a fork until well blended together. Set the bowl aside in a warm spot (not in a hot spot like the oven, or the eggs will cook).

Cook the pasta al dente (see page 13), and drain, leaving it quite wet. Add the pasta to the eggs in the bowl,

continued

stirring vigorously so that the eggs cover the hot pasta *without scrambling*. Add the pancetta-wine mixture to the pasta mixture and toss well again. Serve immediately, passing the additional cheese at the table.

MACCHERONI CON LA CAPULIATA
MACARONI WITH GROUND MEAT serves 4

Capuliata is Sicilian for "chopped beef," which is quite a treat for Sicilians. Because beef is not produced to any degree in Sicily, their consumption runs more to fish, game, pork, kid, and chicken. This is a hearty dish, satisfying to both soul and body; it makes a wonderful one-dish supper. SUGGESTED WINES: CABERNET SAUVIGNON OR MERLOT

NOTE: In Sicily this dish is often prepared as described and, when completed, put into a well-oiled casserole. The top is liberally sprinkled with more cheese, and the dish is then baked in a preheated 450°F oven for about 20 minutes. It is served very hot.

¼ **cup extra virgin olive oil**

1 **onion, finely chopped**

1 **large clove garlic, finely chopped**

8 **ounces (or a little more) ground chuck or other beef**

½ **cup red wine**

Place the oil and onion in a large, heavy skillet over medium heat and gently sauté the onion until just soft, about 3 minutes. Add the garlic and sauté until golden, about 1 minute. Add the meat and cook, stirring to break up any lumps, until it just loses its redness, about 5 minutes. Add the wine and cook for about 10 minutes more. Add the parsley, basil, tomatoes, salt,

- 3 tablespoons chopped fresh Italian parsley
- 2 tablespoons chopped fresh basil leaves, or 1 teaspoon dried
- 1 pound fresh tomatoes, cored, peeled, and finely chopped, or 1 (14-ounce) can tomatoes, chopped, including juice (about 2 cups)

Sea salt and freshly ground black pepper

Pinch of red pepper flakes

- 8 ounces dried penne, rigatoni, or other short, stubby pasta
- 3/4 cup grated provolone or caciocavallo cheese, plus additional for passing

pepper, and red pepper flakes and simmer for about 20 minutes.

Have a heated serving bowl ready. When the sauce is almost done, cook the pasta al dente (see page 13), and drain well. Place the pasta in the serving bowl and mix it with half the sauce and half the cheese. Top with the rest of the sauce and cheese. Serve it very hot and pass the additional cheese at the table.

PAGLIA E FIENO STRAW AND HAY PASTA serves 4 to 6

This is one of the times that I believe spinach pasta is justified. The color contrast in this dish is lovely, and the flavor is so good that it puts the recipe in a class by itself. Making fresh spinach pasta is described on page 11, or you can buy it fresh or dried. SUGGESTED WINES: PINOT BIANCO OR VERDICCHIO

$^1/_4$ cup unsalted butter

1   yellow onion, finely diced

8   ounces boiled ham, or
    5 ounces prosciutto di
    Parma, shredded

$^2/_3$ cup fresh or frozen tiny
    peas (thawed)

1   cup heavy cream

Sea salt and freshly ground
    black pepper

3 or 4 generous gratings of
    fresh nutmeg

7   ounces plain fresh
    tagliarini (tagliolini), or
    6 ounces dried

7   ounces fresh green spinach
    tagliarini, or 6 ounces
    dried

$^3/_4$ cup freshly grated
    Parmesan cheese, plus
    additional for passing

Melt the butter in a heavy skillet over medium-low heat. Add the onion and sauté until translucent, 5 to 6 minutes. Add the ham and sauté for about 3 minutes, or until hot. Add the peas and stir well for about 1 minute, or until warmed through. Add the cream and cook 5 more minutes to allow the cream to thicken a little. Season with salt, pepper, and nutmeg. Keep warm.

Have a heated serving bowl ready. Cook the pasta al dente (see page 13), and drain well. Put the pasta in the serving bowl. Add half the sauce and half the cheese and mix very well. Top with the remaining sauce and cheese. Serve immediately, and pass more cheese at the table if you wish.

SPAGHETTI ALLA VIAREGGINA

SPAGHETTI WITH CLAMS AND TOMATO serves 4 to 6

This very popular dish from Viareggio in Tuscany is equally at home in Rome, Naples, and Sicily. Even people who do not ordinarily care much for clams will eat this recipe with gusto. SUGGESTED WINES: PINOT GRIGIO OR VERDICCHIO

3 pounds small clams in their shells, or 2 (7-ounce) cans chopped clams in their juice

1/3 cup extra virgin olive oil

3 large cloves garlic, finely chopped

1/3 cup dry white wine

1 pound fresh tomatoes, cored, peeled, and chopped, or 1 (14-ounce) can tomatoes, chopped, including juice (about 2 cups)

Sea salt and plenty of freshly ground black pepper

Generous pinch of red pepper flakes

12 ounces dried spaghetti or linguine

1/3 cup chopped fresh Italian parsley

Wash the clams' shells well, scrubbing them with a brush to remove the sand and debris. Put the oil and garlic in a large, heavy skillet over medium heat. Brown the garlic well, but do not burn, 1 to 2 minutes. Add the wine, tomatoes, and clams in their shells. Taste for salt and add more as needed. Cook over high heat for 2 minutes. Add the black pepper and red pepper flakes and cook until the clams are open and the sauce is slightly thickened. Do not overcook the clams. (Alternatively, if using canned clams, add them with their juices when you add the black pepper and pepper flakes. Cook for 3 to 4 minutes, until heated through.)

Have a heated serving bowl ready. Cook the spaghetti al dente (see page 13), and drain well. Place the pasta in the serving bowl. Add half the sauce and mix well. Top with the remaining sauce, sprinkle on the parsley, and serve. Please, no cheese with this dish.

RIGATONCINI AL BASILICO E PANNA
SMALL RIGATONI WITH BASIL AND CREAM serves 6

This rich and tasty pasta makes a great first course or small meal. If you make the sauce a day or two ahead, you could make this dish for a buffet without much last-minute rush. SUGGESTED WINES: PINOT GRIGIO OR CABERNET SAUVIGNON

3 ounces pancetta, sliced ¼ inch thick and cut into small dice

1 tablespoon extra virgin olive oil

5 ounces unsalted butter

2 cloves garlic, finely chopped

3 ounces brandy

1 cup heavy cream

1 large fresh tomato, cored, peeled, and finely diced

1 teaspoon red pepper flakes

Sea salt and freshly ground black pepper

12 or more leaves fresh basil, julienned or chopped

12 ounces dried rigatoncini or similar stubby pasta

1¼ cups freshly grated pecorino cheese, plus additional for passing

Put the pancetta and oil in a heavy skillet over medium heat and sauté until the meat is slightly crispy and golden, about 2 minutes. Drain any excess fat and then add the butter and garlic. Sauté the garlic until it is golden, about 2 minutes. Add the brandy and flame it—*be careful!* Add the cream, tomato, pepper flakes, salt, and pepper, and let everything simmer on medium heat for about 5 minutes. Add the basil and stir. The cream mixture should be thick but still liquid enough to use as a sauce. Keep warm.

Have individual heated plates ready. Cook the pasta al dente (see page 13). Drain it, but be sure to save 4 to 6 tablespoons of the cooking water to thin the sauce, if necessary. Toss the pasta with the sauce in the skillet or use a heated bowl. Serve on the heated plates and top with the 1¼ cups grated cheese. Pass the additional cheese at the table.

SPAGHETTI ALLA PUTTANESCA HOOKER'S PASTA

serves 4 to 6

No one seems to know why this pasta was named after the ladies in the world's oldest profession. Perhaps the fact that it can be eaten cold explains it—they could cook, do some business, and have a nice cold meal ready. But at room temperature it could be a tasty meal on a hot day when you want a "do-ahead" dish. SUGGESTED WINES: LACRYMA CHRISTI DEL VESUVIO OR CHIANTI CLASSICO

2 to 3 tablespoons extra virgin olive oil

2 cloves garlic, minced

2 ounces or more kalamata or Gaeta olives, pitted and coarsely chopped

1 teaspoon drained, coarsely chopped capers

1 large fresh tomato, cored, peeled, and coarsely chopped

4 or 5 anchovy fillets, coarsely chopped

12 ounces dried spaghetti

1/3 cup finely chopped fresh Italian parsley

Sea salt and freshly ground black pepper

Place the oil and garlic in a skillet over medium heat and sauté until the garlic is golden, about 1 minute. Add the olives, capers, tomato, and anchovy fillets. Stir well and heat through for about 6 minutes; keep the sauce warm.

Have a heated serving bowl ready. Cook the pasta al dente (see page 13), and drain well. Place the pasta in the serving bowl and add half the sauce. Toss well. Top with the remaining sauce and sprinkle on the parsley, salt, and pepper. Serve hot. Please, no cheese with this dish.

MINESTRA DI DITALINI E CAVOLFIORE
DITALINI PASTA WITH CAULIFLOWER serves 6

My mother made this on cold, mournful days, and mostly we ate it in silence, letting the heat from the pasta build up inside until we broke a little sweat. It was almost mystical. Leftovers are delicious as a cold soup eaten with intermittent bites of radishes and young stalks of celery. SUGGESTED WINES: VERDICCHIO OR REGALEALI ROSSO

1 large head cauliflower, trimmed of outer leaves

6 teaspoons sea salt

3 tablespoons (or more) extra virgin olive oil

1 large yellow onion, finely chopped

2 large cloves garlic, finely chopped

$\frac{1}{2}$ teaspoon (or more) red pepper flakes (I like more)

$\frac{1}{2}$ teaspoon (or more) freshly ground black pepper

12 ounces dried ditalini or similar short, stubby pasta

1 cup freshly grated aged pecorino cheese, for sprinkling

Cut the cauliflower, including the stem, into small pieces. In a large pot, bring 4 quarts of water with 4 teaspoons of the salt to a boil over medium-high heat. Add the cauliflower and boil for about 4 minutes, until just tender; drain the cauliflower and transfer to a dish or bowl, reserving the water for boiling the pasta. (This can all be done a few hours ahead.)

In a large, heavy skillet heat about 1 tablespoon of the oil over medium heat. Add the onion and sauté until translucent, about 5 or 6 minutes. Add the garlic and sauté until fragrant, about 2 minutes. Add the pepper flakes, black pepper, and the remaining 2 teaspoons salt. Set aside.

Bring the cauliflower water to a boil again, add the pasta, and stir well. Cook the pasta al dente (see page 13). Drain it, discarding all but $1\frac{1}{2}$ cups of the water (or reserve the remainder to use as a base for vegetable soup). Add the pasta and about $^{1}/_{3}$ cup of the reserved pasta water to the skillet with the onion mixture. Stir over medium heat until the pasta is cooked a bit more and almost ready to eat, about 2 to 3 minutes, then add the cauliflower and stir well until it is very hot. Add a bit more of the remaining pasta water as needed. The dish should be very moist but not soup-like.

Sprinkle with the cheese. Drizzle with the remaining 2 tablespoons of oil, or more as you like, and serve.

PASTA ARRIMINATA

PASTA WITH BROCCOLI "STIRRED AROUND" serves 6

This dish is representative of the ingenious flavors and textures of Sicilian cuisine, which is certainly the most complex of all the Italian regional cuisines. This dish is exotic and delicious. SUGGESTED WINE: ALCAMO BIANCO

1 bunch broccoli or 1 head cauliflower (or a mixture of both), trimmed and cut into pieces about 1½ by 1½ inches

⅓ cup extra virgin olive oil

1 large yellow onion, finely diced

3 anchovy fillets, chopped

½ cup seedless golden or sultana raisins

⅓ cup pine nuts

Small pinch of saffron

Sea salt and freshly ground black pepper

12 ounces dried fusilli, macaroni (such as rigatoni, penne, large shells), or large elbows

½ cup (or more) freshly grated pecorino cheese, for sprinkling

Bring a large pot of salted water to a boil over medium-high heat. Blanch the broccoli until it is just tender, 5 to 6 minutes. Do not overcook. Drain, cool, and set aside.

Place the oil and onion in a large, heavy skillet over medium heat. Sauté the onion until golden, about 5 minutes. Add the broccoli, anchovy fillets, raisins, pine nuts, saffron, salt, and pepper. Reduce the heat and cook gently until the flavors are well blended, about 5 minutes. Keep warm.

Cook the pasta al dente (see page 13). Drain it except for ¼ cup of the cooking water. Add the sauce and stir well. Sprinkle on the cheese. Serve hot.

FETTUCCINE AL VODKA FETTUCCINE WITH VODKA

serves 6

Sometimes I love this with penne or rigatoncini, and once in a while, squid-ink pasta. It is one of the all-time favorites at my restaurant, Vivande. SUGGESTED WINES: PINOT GRIGIO OR ARNEIS

3 ounces pancetta, sliced ¼ inch thick and cut into small dice

1 tablespoon extra virgin olive oil

Sea salt

2 fresh tomatoes, cored, peeled, and finely diced

1 pound fresh fettuccine, or 12 ounces dried

1 bunch green onions, white and green parts, sliced diagonally into 1-inch pieces

⅓ cup vodka

1 cup freshly grated Parmesan cheese, for sprinkling, plus additional for passing

Coarsely ground black pepper, for sprinkling

Put the pancetta and oil in a large, heavy skillet. Sauté over medium heat until the pancetta is golden and slightly crunchy, about 2 minutes. Add some salt. Remove from the heat and add the tomatoes.

Have individual heated plates ready. Cook the pasta al dente (see page 13), and drain, leaving a bit of water on the pasta. Meanwhile, reheat the sauce, add the green onions, remove the pan from the heat, and carefully add the vodka. Stir well, and let some of the alcohol evaporate, about 1½ minutes. *Never add the vodka while the sauce is on a heat source because it could flare up and startle or injure you.* Add the pasta to the sauce and toss well.

Serve on the heated plates, sprinkling on plenty of the cheese and black pepper. Pass the additional cheese at the table.

PAPPARDELLE CON I PORCINI
PAPPARDELLE WITH PORCINI MUSHROOMS serves 6

If you can find fresh porcini mushrooms (*Boletus edulis*), use them to make this epicurean dish. Dried porcini, which are readily available in food stores, are a good substitute. SUGGESTED WINES: CORVO ROSSO OR REGALEALI ROSSO

- 12 ounces (or more) fresh porcini mushrooms, or 1 ounce dried
- 3 ounces pancetta, sliced ¼ inch thick and cut into small dice
- 2 tablespoons extra virgin olive oil

Sea salt and freshly ground black pepper

- 2 large cloves garlic, finely chopped
- 1 fresh tomato, cored, peeled, and cut into small dice
- 1 cup dry white wine
- 1 pound fresh pappardelle, or 12 ounces dried
- ¼ cup coarsely chopped fresh Italian parsley

Generous pinch of red pepper flakes, for sprinkling

Clean the fresh porcini with a small brush or wipe with a clean kitchen towel. (Do not wash them in water, because they get waterlogged easily.) If you use dried porcini, soak them for 20 minutes in enough warm water to cover by at least 3 inches. Wring out as much water as you can, leave them in large pieces, and strain the soaking water to remove any debris and sand. (Use the flavored water in other dishes such as sauces or as a base for soup—do not waste it.)

Put the pancetta and oil in a large, heavy skillet. Sauté over medium heat until the pancetta is golden, about 2 minutes. Add the mushrooms, salt, and pepper to the pancetta. Sauté, stirring, until golden, about 3 minutes. Add the garlic and cook for about 1 minute. Add the tomato and white wine, stir well, and cook for about 5 minutes. Keep warm.

continued

Have individual heated plates ready. Cook the pasta al dente (see page 13), and drain, leaving it wet. Be sure the sauce is hot, then add the pasta and parsley and toss well together. Serve immediately on the heated plates, sprinkling on the pepper flakes.

PAPPARDELLE AL RADICCHIO SALTATO
PAPPARDELLE WITH SAUTÉED RADICCHIO serves 6

Pappardelle are 1-inch-wide, flat noodles as thin as fettuccine, usually made fresh and hand-cut. You may substitute fettuccine if necessary. SUGGESTED WINES: ALCAMO BIANCO OR VALPOLICELLA

5 ounces (or more or less) pancetta, sliced ¼ inch thick and finely chopped

3 tablespoons extra virgin olive oil

2 large red onions, coarsely cut into ½-inch dice

2 heads radicchio di Chioggia (round heads)

Sea salt and plenty of freshly ground black pepper

1 pound fresh pappardelle, or 12 ounces dried

Put the pancetta in a large, heavy skillet over medium heat. When the fat melts, sauté the pancetta until it is light golden, about 5 minutes. Remove the pancetta with a slotted spoon and discard all the fat. Wipe the pan clean, add a tablespoon or so of the olive oil, and sauté the onions until soft with little scorch marks here and there, about 5 minutes. Set aside in a bowl.

Trim the radicchio and remove the old or soft outer leaves. Trim out some of the stem and discard it. Coarsely chop the radicchio into 1-inch pieces. Add the remaining 2 tablespoons of oil to the skillet and sauté the radicchio over medium heat until it is tender, but not too soft, about 6 minutes. Combine all the sautéed ingredients and season with salt and pepper

Have individual heated plates ready. Cook the pasta until al dente (see page 13), making sure the other ingredients are hot when the pasta is almost done. Drain the pasta, but leave about 2 to 3 tablespoons of water in it, and return it to the pot. Mix the pasta with the sautéed pancetta, onions, and radicchio. Serve on the heated plates. No cheese, please.

FETTUCCINE ALLA GIOVANNI
JOHN'S FETTUCCINE WITH SMOKED SAUSAGE serves 6

One day I was hungrier than usual and wanted more than just my own house-made, house-smoked smoked sausage. This has become one of my bestselling dishes—and all because I was famished! Do not use a heavily smoked sausage.

SUGGESTED WINES: ALCAMO BIANCO OR CANNONAU DI SARDEGNA

4 to 5 links (about 1 to 1¹/₂ pounds) lightly smoked sausage

4 tablespoons extra virgin olive oil

3 cloves garlic, finely chopped

Sea salt and lots of freshly ground black pepper

1 cup dry white wine

1 fresh tomato, cored, peeled, and finely chopped

1 small bunch (about 1 pound) spinach, well trimmed

1 pound fresh spinach or plain fettuccine, or 12 ounces dried

1 teaspoon red pepper flakes, for sprinkling

You can cook the sausages either in the oven or on the stovetop. To cook in the oven, preheat the oven to 375°F. Rest a wire rack over a roasting pan. Set the sausage links on the rack and roast for about 30 minutes. To cook in a pan, put the sausage links in a large, heavy skillet, add about 1 cup of water, cover, and simmer over medium heat for about 15 minutes. Discard any water and sauté the sausages until they are golden brown and done, about 10 minutes.

In either case, cool the links and cut them into large chunks (about 6 pieces per link).

Put the sausage pieces in a large, heavy skillet over medium heat and add a little oil, the garlic, and some salt and pepper. Sauté until the sausage is hot and the garlic is golden, about 2 minutes. Pour in the white

continued

wine to stop the garlic from cooking. Add the tomato and continue to cook until most of the wine has evaporated, about 4 minutes. Add the spinach and cook for about 2 minutes, until it has just collapsed.

Have individual heated plates ready. Cook the pasta al dente (see page 13) and drain, being sure that it is still wet. Transfer the pasta to the skillet with the sauce and toss well to mix everything. Serve the hot pasta on the heated plates, and sprinkle the pepper flakes over the top.

FUSILLI ALLA CARLO FUSILLI AS CARLO MAKES IT

serves 6

One day I just started combining ingredients and came up with this dish for my lunch. Eight people spotted it and wanted it. *Ecco*, a dish was born. It is by far the most popular dish we regularly do on my Vivande menu.

SUGGESTED WINES: CHIANTI OR AGLIANICO

5 tablespoons pine nuts

3 ounces pancetta, sliced $^1/_4$ inch thick and cut into small dice

5 tablespoons extra virgin olive oil

To toast the pine nuts, place a small, heavy skillet over medium heat. In about $1^1/_2$ minutes, add the pine nuts (but no fat) and immediately reduce the heat to low. Stir the pine nuts constantly to toast them evenly, about 5 minutes. Watch carefully because they burn

5   ounces unsalted butter

5   ounces button mushrooms,
    sliced medium-thin

Sea salt and freshly ground
    black pepper

1   large fresh tomato, cored,
    peeled, and finely diced

1   cup heavy cream

12 ounces dried fusilli

$^1/_3$ cup freshly grated
    Parmesan cheese

1   cup grated pecorino
    cheese, plus additional for
    passing

easily. When they are done, immediately pour them into a cool dish or bowl, which stops the cooking.

Put the pancetta and oil in a heavy skillet and sauté over medium heat until the pancetta is slightly crispy and golden, about 2 minutes. Drain any excess fat, then add the butter, mushrooms, salt, pepper, toasted pine nuts, and tomato, and sauté for about 2 minutes. Add the cream and reduce for about 4 minutes. Stir in the Parmesan. Keep warm over low heat.

Have individual heated plates ready. Cook the pasta al dente (see page 13), and drain, saving 4 to 6 tablespoons of the water. Toss the pasta with the sauce. If the sauce is too thick, add 1 or more tablespoons of the reserved pasta water. Serve on the heated plates and top with the pecorino cheese, passing more at the table.

FETTUCCINE CON POMODORI SCOPPIATI

FETTUCCINE WITH BURST TOMATOES serves 6

Scoppiato means "burst" or "exploded," and of course this happens when you put tiny tomatoes into a hot pan. SUGGESTED WINES: MERLOT OR MONTEPULCIANO D'ABRUZZO

1 large red bell pepper, or ½ yellow and ½ orange bell peppers

5 tablespoons extra virgin olive oil

2 large cloves garlic, well crushed

Sea salt and freshly ground black pepper

1 pound (or more) mixed yellow and red cherry tomatoes, stemmed

1 pound fresh fettuccine, or 12 ounces dried

¼ cup coarsely chopped fresh Italian parsley

6 ounces imported provolone cheese, finely diced

1 teaspoon (or more) red pepper flakes, for sprinkling

With tongs, hold the bell pepper directly over a gas flame until it becomes almost black. When the skin is blistered all over, remove the pepper from the heat and let it cool, uncovered, on a plate. When cool, peel off the skin with a paring knife or your fingers, split the pepper open, and scrape off the seeds and remove the stem. Do not wash it with water because it diminishes the flavor. (Little black spots are normal and desirable on fire-roasted peppers.) If you use a broiler, cut the pepper into quarters, stem, scrape off the seeds, and place the skin side as close to the heat source as possible. Proceed as directed. When the pepper is skinned, cut it into ½-inch dice.

Put the oil in a large, heavy skillet over medium heat. Add the garlic and salt and pepper, and sauté the garlic until golden, about 1 minute. Add the bell pepper and sauté until hot, 1 to 2 minutes. Add the tomatoes and

continued

sauté until they soften a bit and start exploding, about 5 minutes or less.

Have individual heated plates ready. Cook the pasta al dente (see page 13). Make sure the sauce is hot when the pasta is almost done. Add the parsley and provolone cheese to the sauce and stir. Drain the pasta, leaving it slightly wet. Add it to the pan of sauce and mix well. Serve the pasta on the heated plates and sprinkle with the pepper flakes.

TAGLIATELLE ALLA BOLOGNESE
THIN RIBBON PASTA WITH BOLOGNA-STYLE SAUCE

serves 4

This classic pasta from Bologna, considered by many to be the food capital of northern Italy, is best eaten in its hometown, but you can achieve delicious results here if you don't over-sauce it. SUGGESTED WINES: ARNEIS OR VALPOLICELLA

2^1/$_2$ cups Salsa Bolognese (Bolognese Meat Sauce, page 21)

12 (or more) ounces fresh tagliatelle, or 8 ounces dried

^{1}/$_2$ cup (or more) freshly grated Parmesan cheese, for passing

Heat the sauce in a heavy saucepan and keep it hot.

Have a heated serving plate ready. Cook the pasta al dente (see page 13), and drain well. Return it to the cooking pot, add a little of the sauce, and mix thoroughly. Serve on the serving plate with a ladleful of sauce on top. Pass the cheese at the table.

FETTUCCINE CON PUMATE E GALLINACCI

FETTUCCINE WITH SUN-DRIED TOMATOES AND CHANTERELLES serves 6

Sun-dried tomatoes (*pumate*) were developed by the Italians as a way to preserve vine-ripened tomatoes for sauce-making during the harsh winter and early spring months. SUGGESTED WINES: ORVIETO OR VERDICCHIO

6   ounces sun-dried tomatoes, or 4 ounces dehydrated tomatoes

5   ounces unsalted butter

1   small yellow onion, finely chopped

Sea salt

8   ounces chanterelle mushrooms, cleaned and coarsely chopped

1   cup (or a bit more) heavy cream

1   pound fresh fettuccine, or 12 ounces dried

Freshly ground black pepper, for sprinkling

Rehydrate the tomatoes by soaking them in boiling water about 5 minutes, but be careful not to disintegrate them by soaking for too long. Drain, dry, and chop into small pieces; set aside in a bowl.

Put the butter in a large, heavy skillet over medium heat. When it melts, add the onion and salt. Sauté until the onion is translucent, about 5 minutes. Add the chopped tomatoes, then the mushrooms, and sauté until the mushrooms are tender, about 5 minutes. Add the cream and reduce for 3 or 4 minutes.

Have individual heated plates ready. Cook the pasta al dente (see page 13) and drain, leaving it slightly wet. If you have made the sauce ahead, reheat it now. Add the cooked pasta and toss well. Serve on the heated plates and top with plenty of pepper. No cheese, please.

PENNE ALLA PRIMAVERA
PENNE PASTA FOR SPRINGTIME serves 6

The idea is to use as many different vegetables as you like, simply prepared and mixed in with pasta. This is an ideal dish for the vegan family or friends, because you can use packaged pasta, which is usually made from just semolina and water (no eggs). SUGGESTED WINES: PINOT BIANCO OR VALPOLICELLA

1 pound (or more) red, green, or yellow bell peppers or a mixture of all three

5 tablespoons (or more) extra virgin olive oil

3 small zucchini, cut into ¼-inch-thick slices

6 ounces button or cremini mushrooms, chopped medium-coarse

3 large cloves garlic, finely chopped

2 large fresh tomatoes (about 12 ounces), cored, peeled, and chopped medium-coarse

Sea salt

12 ounces dried penne or similar pasta

Freshly ground black pepper, for sprinkling

Core the bell peppers, discard the seeds, and cut them into ¼-inch-thick slices. Put 2 tablespoons of the olive oil in a large, heavy skillet over medium heat and sauté the peppers until they are barely soft and have not begun to brown, 5 to 6 minutes. Add the zucchini, and sauté for about 2 minutes. Add the mushrooms and garlic, and cook another 2 minutes, stirring frequently. Stir in the tomatoes and turn off the heat. Add some salt.

Have individual heated plates ready. Cook the pasta al dente (see page 13), and drain, leaving it wet. Heat the sauce, if it has cooled, mix in the pasta, and serve on the heated plates. Sprinkle on lots of pepper and drizzle on the remaining 3 tablespoons of oil. This pasta is also good served at room temperature.

MACCHERONI CON BOCCONCINI
MACARONI WITH SMALL MOZZARELLA BALLS serves 6

This dish is a genuine taste sensation. *Bocconcini* literally means "mouthfuls" or "little bites" of mozzarella cheese. The cheese will be very stringy, so it is a little challenging to eat, but fun! SUGGESTED WINES: CHIANTI CLASSICO OR MONTEPULCIANO D'ABRUZZO

¼ cup extra virgin olive oil

1 pound fresh tomatoes, cored, peeled, and chopped medium-coarse

Sea salt and freshly ground black pepper

1 pound of any dried short, stubby pasta such as ciufetti, penne, conchiglie, rigatoncini, or chifferi

8 ounces bocconcini, each halved

1 cup fresh or frozen tiny peas (thawed)

1 cup (or more) freshly grated Parmesan cheese, for sprinkling

⅓ bunch basil, julienned

Put the oil in a large, heavy skillet over medium heat and add the tomatoes. Season with salt and pepper, and sauté until the tomatoes collapse a bit, about 4 minutes.

Have individual heated plates ready. Cook the pasta al dente (see page 13), and drain, leaving it wet. Add the bocconcini and peas to the sauce and toss. Mix in the pasta and toss well again. Serve on very hot plates. Sprinkle on generous amounts of the grated cheese, and sprinkle the basil all over the top. Eat the pasta while very hot.

TAGLIATELLE CON OSTRICHE
TAGLIATELLE PASTA WITH OYSTERS serves 6

Shellfish lovers really like this dish. It is very tasty, briny, and reminds one of the seashore. If you don't shuck your own oysters, use jarred ones from a reliable fishmonger. SUGGESTED WINES: CIRÒ ROSATO OR VERMENTINO

5 ounces unsalted butter

3 cloves garlic, finely chopped

1 cup dry white wine

Sea salt and freshly ground black pepper

1 pound fresh tagliatelle, spaghettini, linguine, or capellini, or 12 ounces dried

4 green onions, white and green parts, cut into ¹/₂-inch pieces

24 small or 18 medium shucked oysters

¹/₄ bunch spinach, trimmed

1 tablespoon (or so) freshly squeezed lemon juice

Put the butter in a large, heavy skillet over medium heat and add the garlic. Sauté until the garlic becomes light golden and fragrant, about 1 minute. Add the wine, and let it reduce for about 3 minutes. Season with salt and pepper, and keep warm.

Cook the pasta al dente (see page 13), and drain, leaving it slightly wet. Have heated plates ready.

Meanwhile, add the green onions, oysters, spinach, and lemon juice to the sauce. Let simmer for about 2 minutes. Add the pasta to the sauce and toss well.

Serve immediately on the heated plates. Sprinkle on plenty more pepper.

VARIATION: For a rich variation, use ¹/₂ cup wine and add 1 cup of heavy cream; let the sauce reduce for about 3 minutes over medium heat, and proceed as directed.

PASTA
OTHER
WAYS

pasta altri sensi

RAVIOLI STUFFED PASTA PILLOWS serves 8

The word for this dish comes from the Genovese *robiole,* meaning "rubbish," or in our case, leftovers. Use your imagination and make your own version. It is very difficult to make an "authentic" ravioli stuffing because it is so often determined by what is at hand. You may substitute the same quantity (and quality) of ground chicken and veal for the meats used in this recipe. All kinds of rollers, molds, and forms are available to help you shape and seal the ravioli. If you plan to make them frequently, you may find some of these utensils useful. SUGGESTED WINES: CABERNET SAUVIGNON OR VINO NOBILE DI MONTEPULCIANO

2   tablespoons extra virgin olive oil

8   ounces ground pork

8   ounces ground beef

2   ounces prosciutto di Parma or mortadella, finely ground

4   ounces best-quality boiled ham, finely ground (¹/₂ cup)

1   clove garlic, minced

2   generous gratings of fresh nutmeg

¹/₂ cup freshly grated Parmesan cheese, plus additional for passing

To make the filling, in a large, heavy skillet heat the oil over medium heat. Add the pork and beef, and gently cook until the meat loses its red color (unless you are already using cooked leftover meat), about 6 minutes. Set aside to cool. When the meat is cool, combine with the prosciutto, boiled ham, garlic, nutmeg, cheese, salt, pepper, and eggs and blend all into a smooth paste. Transfer to a bowl and set aside.

Flour a clean kitchen towel or cloth. To assemble the ravioli, divide the pasta dough into 4 equal pieces. (You will need 2 broad sheets of pasta to make each sheet of ravioli.) Roll out 1 piece of pasta dough into a sheet no more than ¹/₁₆ inch thick (thinner is even better).

continued

Sea salt and freshly ground
black pepper

2 large eggs, beaten, plus
more for sealing, if needed

3-egg pasta dough (see page
5), covered with plastic
wrap (about 1 pound)

4 cups Salsa al Pomodoro
(Quick Tomato Sauce,
page 19)

Keep the remaining 3 pieces of dough covered with plastic wrap while you work with the first piece. (Do not dry the pasta; for stuffed pasta, the dough must stick to itself.) Immediately begin to place the filling, 1 tablespoon at a time, in even rows across and down the sheet of pasta, about $1^1/_2$ inches apart. Roll a second sheet of pasta the same size and thickness as the first. Place the second sheet on top of the first, and, with your fingers, press down between the mounds of filling to form ravioli squares. Cut out the squares, following the pressed lines, with a crimped pastry cutter. If the pasta is a little dry, moisten the edges with additional beaten egg or water to help seal the dough. Set the ravioli aside to rest on the floured cloth. Do not pile them up, because they will stick to each other. Repeat with the remaining pasta dough.

Have a heated serving dish ready. Just before serving, cook the ravioli al dente (see page 13). Meanwhile, heat the sauce. Drain the ravioli well, and lay them in the heated dish. Pour the sauce on top and serve hot, passing the additional cheese at the table.

TORTELLONI TORTELLONI AS MADE IN TUSCANY

serves 4 to 6

This is an unusual and delicious stuffed pasta, which should only be made fresh. For freezing instructions, see the note on the opposite page. SUGGESTED WINES: BARBERA OR CHIANTI RISERVA

NOTE: You can freeze uncooked tortellini and other small stuffed pastas like ravioli, cappelletti, agnolotti, pansotti, and tortelloni. Just put them in a single layer on a baking sheet and freeze. When they are frozen, pack in jars or self-sealing plastic bags for later use; they keep well for up to 6 months. When ready to cook, drop them into boiling water while they are still frozen. Add 1 minute to the cooking time.

8 ounces finely ground pork with some fat

3 to 4 tablespoons dry white wine

Sea salt and freshly ground black pepper

1 large clove garlic, minced

3 to 4 tablespoons minced fresh Italian parsley

1 to 2 tablespoons tomato paste

1¼ cups freshly grated Parmesan cheese

3 to 4 tablespoons dried unflavored bread crumbs

To make the filling, in a large, heavy skillet cook the pork over medium heat until it just loses its pink color, about 6 minutes. Add the wine and cook for about 2 minutes more. Set aside to cool. When cool, add the salt, pepper, garlic, parsley, tomato paste, ¼ cup of the cheese, the bread crumbs, eggs, and red pepper flakes, and mix well.

Flour a clean kitchen towel or cloth. To assemble the tortelloni, divide the pasta dough into 4 equal pieces and roll and fill as instructed for making ravioli (see page 77). Roll the sheets no more than ¹⁄₁₆ inch thick

continued

2 large eggs, beaten, plus more for sealing, if needed

Generous pinch of red pepper flakes

3-egg pasta dough (see page 5), covered with plastic wrap (about 1 pound)

1 cup unsalted butter

8 to 10 fresh sage leaves, torn into thirds

Freshly ground black pepper, for sprinkling

and place the filling $2^1/_2$ inches apart. With your fingers, press down between the mounds of filling to form large squares, about $2^1/_2$ by $2^1/_2$ inches. Cut out the squares, following the pressed lines with a crimped pastry cutter. If the pasta is a little dry, moisten the edges with additional beaten egg or water to help seal the dough. Set the tortelloni aside to rest on the floured cloth. Do not pile them up, because they will stick to each other. Repeat with the remaining pasta dough.

Have a heated serving dish ready. Cook the tortelloni al dente (see page 13). While the tortelloni cook, make the sauce. In a heavy skillet, melt the butter over *very* low heat; do not cook. When melted, add the sage leaves and stir well. Keep hot.

Drain the tortelloni. Put a little of the sauce on the bottom of the heated dish. Add a layer of tortelloni, then sauce, and then some of the remaining grated cheese, and repeat until you end up with butter sauce and cheese on top. Top with black pepper and serve hot.

AGNOLOTTI ROUND STUFFED PASTA "LAMBS"

serves 6

Agnolotti ("little lambs"), in case you haven't guessed, are ravioli in sheep's clothing. So many Italian names are whimsical and express someone's imagination, adding to the maddening confusion of trying to identify and codify Italian dishes. Thank heaven they are so delicious! An error in name will still get you a gastronomic treat. For freezing instructions, see the note on page 78. SUGGESTED WINES: VALPOLICELLA OR CORVO ROSSO

2   **bunches spinach, trimmed**

½ **cup unsalted butter**

1   **small yellow onion, finely diced**

8   **ounces ground beef**

1   **slice mortadella, finely chopped**

½ **cup freshly grated Parmesan cheese**

Sea salt and freshly ground black pepper

2   **large eggs, beaten, plus more for sealing, if needed**

3-egg pasta dough (see page 5), covered with plastic wrap (about 1 pound)

4   **cups Salsa di Pomodoro Stracotto (Slow Tomato Sauce, page 18)**

To make the filling, wash the spinach, shake off the excess water, and steam it in a covered pot over medium heat, using only the water left on the leaves. When it has just collapsed, about 2 minutes, remove the lid and let it dry out a bit over low heat. Set it aside to cool.

Melt the butter in a heavy skillet over medium-low heat. Add the onion and sauté just until it is translucent, about 5 minutes. Add the beef and cook just until it loses its red color, 5 to 6 minutes. Set aside to cool.

Combine the mortadella, ¼ cup of the Parmesan, the salt and pepper, and the eggs. Combine with the cooled spinach and beef; blend well.

Flour a clean kitchen towel or cloth. To assemble the agnolotti, divide the pasta dough into 4 equal pieces and roll and fill as instructed for making ravioli (see page 77). With your fingers, press down all around the mounds of filling in a circular shape. Cut out the agnolotti by placing the mouth of a shot glass, a round cookie cutter, or an agnolotti cutter over the circular seal and pressing. If the pasta is a little dry, moisten the edges with additional beaten egg or water to help seal the dough. Set the agnolotti aside to rest on the floured cloth. Do not pile them up because they will stick to each other. Repeat with the remaining pasta dough.

Have a heated serving dish ready. Just before serving, cook the agnolotti al dente (see page 13). Meanwhile, heat the sauce. Drain the agnolotti, transfer to the heated dish, cover with sauce, and serve. Pass the remaining $1/4$ cup of cheese at the table.

CONCHIGLIE RIPIENI STUFFED PASTA SHELLS

serves 6 to 8

This is an excellent dish for entertaining as it can be assembled in advance, frozen, and cooked or reheated just before serving. A serving of two or three makes a perfect first course; five or six make a main dish. A nice variation is to make two fillings, one with meat and the other with ricotta and spinach. There are about 40 pasta shells in a pound. Some may break—use them in soup. You can easily halve this recipe. SUGGESTED WINES: CABERNET SAUVIGNON OR CHIANTI RISERVA

NOTE: You can totally assemble this dish and freeze it or freeze any extras. However, it should not be thawed before heating because the pasta will become soggy. Freeze it in an ovenproof dish and simply bake it covered (and frozen) in a 350°F oven for about 1 1/2 hours before serving.

4 cups Balsamella (White Sauce, page 22)

2 pounds ricotta

4 ounces prosciutto di Parma, finely minced

1 cup mozzarella cheese, finely diced

1/4 cup finely chopped fresh Italian parsley

2 large eggs

Sea salt and freshly ground black pepper

1 pound dried jumbo pasta shells

Prepare two 9 by 14-inch ovenproof casserole dishes or one large roasting pan by spreading a 1/8-inch layer of Balsamella on the bottom; set aside. Preheat the oven to 350°F.

To make the filling, mix the ricotta, prosciutto, mozzarella, parsley, and eggs together in a bowl. Season with salt and pepper. Set aside.

Have an oiled baking sheet ready. Cook the pasta shells *very* al dente (about 2 minutes less than the package directs). Drain the shells and plunge them into cold

2 cups Salsa al Pomodoro (Quick Tomato Sauce, page 19)

$^1/_2$ cup freshly grated Parmesan or Romano cheese, for sprinkling

water to stop the cooking process. Drain again and place them on the oiled sheet.

To assemble the shells, fill with the ricotta mixture, using a pastry tube. A spoon or knife will work, but that method is very slow. Place the filled shells on the bed of Balsamella, arranging them fairly close together.

Put some more Balsamella on top of the shells, and then drizzle Salsa al Pomodoro over that. Sprinkle the Parmesan on top.

Bake the conchiglie for 40 to 50 minutes, until hot, bubbling, and light golden on top. Serve very hot.

PANSOTTI CON SALSA DI NOCI

PASTA PILLOWS OF RICOTTA WITH WALNUT SAUCE

serves 8

The region of Liguria is famous for its walnuts, and Ligurians love their pesto made with walnuts instead of the usual pine nuts. I would serve this dish first, followed by small amounts of tasty broiled or roasted meat or fowl.

SUGGESTED WINES: A BOLD RED WINE SUCH AS AGLIANICO OR GATTINARA

1   pound fresh Swiss chard

1   bunch watercress (or borage), cut into 3-inch pieces

2   large eggs, plus more for sealing, if needed

²/₃ cup ricotta

¹/₂ cup freshly grated Parmesan cheese, plus additional for passing

2   generous gratings of fresh nutmeg

Sea salt and freshly ground black pepper

4-egg pasta dough (see page 5), covered with plastic wrap (about 1¹/₂ pounds)

To make the filling, wash the chard well in cold water. Shake off the excess water and steam the chard in a covered pan over medium heat just until done—about 7 minutes (it should not be mushy). Drain well. Chop the chard in a food processor fitted with the metal blade. Add the watercress, the 2 eggs, ricotta, the ¹/₂ cup grated Parmesan, nutmeg, and salt and pepper. Blend well in the food processor. If the mixture looks too wet or runny, add a little more grated Parmesan, or 1 tablespoon of dried unflavored bread crumbs. Set aside.

Flour a clean kitchen towel or cloth. To assemble the pansotti, divide the pasta dough into 4 equal pieces and roll and fill as instructed for making ravioli (page 77). With your fingers, press down around the mounds of filling to form triangles. Cut out the pansotti with

8 ounces walnut meats

3 tablespoons pine nuts

1 small clove garlic

3 tablespoons finely chopped fresh Italian parsley

1/3 cup curdled milk (add a few drops of lemon juice to warmed milk and let it stand at room temperature for 15 to 30 minutes)

1/2 cup extra virgin olive oil

a crimped pastry wheel. If the pasta is a little dry, moisten the edges with additional beaten egg or water to help seal the dough. Set the pansotti aside to rest on the floured cloth. Do not pile them up, because they will stick to each other. Repeat with the remaining pasta dough.

To make the sauce, put the walnuts, pine nuts, garlic, and parsley in the work bowl of a food processor fitted with the metal blade and puree into a smooth paste. Add the curdled milk and mix well; then add the oil and blend some more. Set aside.

Have a heated serving dish ready. Cook the pansotti al dente (see page 13). Drain well, and lay them in the heated dish. Add the sauce and toss well. Serve hot, passing the additional grated Parmesan at the table.

CANNELLONI STUFFED LARGE REEDS serves 6

Everyone loves cannelloni. Small ones can be a delicious first course in a large meal and large ones make a whole meal when served with a salad. This recipe calls for both red and white sauces. But you can use just one, if you prefer.

SUGGESTED WINES: VERDICCHIO OR PINOT BIANCO

NOTE: You can prepare the cannelloni up to 1 day ahead. Store, covered, in the refrigerator. Let the cannelloni come to room temperature before baking as directed. For a meatless variation, you can substitute 1 pound of ricotta cheese for the meats.

1	bunch spinach, or 10 ounces frozen chopped spinach (thawed)
2	tablespoons extra virgin olive oil
1	yellow onion, finely chopped
4	ounces ground beef or veal
4	ounces finely chopped mortadella or unsmoked ham
2	generous gratings of fresh nutmeg
1/4	cup freshly grated Parmesan cheese, plus additional for sprinkling
1	large egg, beaten

To make the filling, wash the fresh spinach, shake off the excess water, and steam it in a covered pot over medium heat, using only the water left on the leaves. When it has just collapsed, about 2 minutes, drain it well and chop medium-fine. Set aside.

Put the oil in a large, heavy skillet over medium heat. Add the onion and sauté just until it is translucent, about 5 minutes. Add the beef and mortadella and cook just until the beef loses its red color, 3 to 4 minutes. Add the spinach, nutmeg, and 1/4 cup cheese. Mix thoroughly and let cool. Stir in the egg. Set aside.

To assemble the cannelloni, roll out the pasta in large sheets less than 1/16 inch thick. Cut the sheets into rectangles about 4 by 5 inches (to yield 12 pieces).

3-egg pasta dough (see page 5), covered with plastic wrap (about 1 pound)

8 cups **Salsa al Pomodoro** (Quick Tomato Sauce, page 19)

2 cups **Balsamella** (White Sauce, page 22)

Have clean damp kitchen towels available to keep the pasta moist. Bring a stockpot of water to a boil over medium-high heat, and add some salt. Drop in 2 or 3 pieces of pasta at a time and cook for about 1 minute. Lift them out and plunge into cold water to stop the cooking process. Lay them on the damp towels.

Preheat the oven to 375°F. Generously butter a 9 by 14-inch ovenproof baking dish, or use extra virgin olive oil. Spread a generous row of filling down the long side of each pasta rectangle and roll them up, starting with the long side. Place the filled cannelloni in the baking dish. Do not pack them too tightly in the dish; leave about $1/4$ inch between them to allow for expansion. Spread evenly with both sauces (or just one—your preference). Sprinkle the additional cheese over the top and bake for about 30 minutes. Serve hot.

LASAGNE BAKED FILLED PASTA SHEETS serves 8 or 10

This could very well be the single most popular pasta dish known outside of Italy. I love to eat it, and I am always delighted to be served lasagne when invited out to dinner. If you like, use spinach pasta for a change.

Instead of cutting the pasta into wide noodles, you can cut it the very old-fashioned way, using the crimped cutter to make squarish pieces about 3 by 3 inches or 3 by 4 inches. These pieces were thrown into the layered casserole at random in the way you would deal a deck of cards—still a nice effect today.

SUGGESTED WINES: CABERNET SAUVIGNON OR CHIANTI

5 cups Salsa di Pomodoro Stracotto (Slow Tomato Sauce, page 18 and method at right)

12 ounces ground beef

4 ounces ground pork

1 cup fresh or frozen tiny peas (thawed)

3-egg plain or spinach pasta dough (see page 5 or 11), covered with plastic wrap, or 12 ounces dried lasagne

1 pound ricotta (optional)

1 cup freshly grated Parmesan cheese

1 cup shredded mozzarella cheese

To make the meat sauce, prepare the tomato sauce as directed in the recipe, adding the ground meats with the onion and garlic. Cook until the meats have lost their red color before you proceed with the rest of the sauce. Add the peas to the sauce just before you remove it from the heat.

Butter a rectangular 9 by 14-inch ovenproof baking dish, or use extra virgin olive oil, and set it aside. Preheat the oven to 375°F.

To make the pasta, roll out the dough into large pasta sheets and dry them as directed (see page 9). Then cut them into traditional lasagne strips about 12 inches

continued

long and $1^1/_2$ to 2 inches wide. Or, to save some work, you can cut the sheets to measure the same size as your baking dish. Use a crimped pastry cutter if you want a fancier edge.

Have clean damp kitchen towels available to keep the pasta moist. Cook the pasta *very* al dente (see page 13), a few at a time. Remove them with a slotted spoon and plunge them into cold water to stop the cooking process. Lay them on the damp towels.

To assemble the lasagne, in the prepared baking dish alternate layers of pasta, sauce, and ricotta, ending with pasta and sauce. Sprinkle the Parmesan and mozzarella on top and dot with a bit more sauce. Bake for 40 to 50 minutes, until bubbling and heated through. Cut into squares and serve piping hot.

SFORMATO DI PASTA PASTA CASSEROLE serves 10

A *sformato* simply means "molded," and often it is turned out of its mold and onto a serving platter. This dish makes a luscious and delicate first course, even more elegant in individual ovenproof ramekins. I believe this must be a relatively new recipe because I can't imagine the old-time Italians going to such pains with a perfectly good dish of pasta. SUGGESTED WINES: VERMENTINO OR ARNEIS

1   tablespoon unsalted butter

1   small shallot, finely chopped

8   ounces boiled ham, finely chopped

³/₄ cup freshly grated Parmesan cheese

Sea salt and freshly ground black pepper

Generous grating of fresh nutmeg

2-egg plain or spinach pasta dough (see page 5 or 11), cut as fettuccine (about 12 ounces)

5   large eggs, separated

1   cup Balsamella (White Sauce, page 22)

Melt the butter in a heavy skillet over low heat, add the shallot, and cook until it is translucent, 5 to 6 minutes. Add the ham and stir. Add the cheese, salt, pepper, and nutmeg and stir again. Set aside and let the mixture cool completely.

Butter a 3 to 3¹/₂-quart soufflé dish generously. Preheat the oven to 375°F.

Cook the fettuccine al dente (see page 13), drain well, and let cool. Add the ham mixture, the egg yolks, and the Balsamella to the pasta. Mix together thoroughly.

With an electric mixer and whisk attachment, beat the egg whites until they are stiff and shiny. Fold them carefully into the pasta mixture and pour into the soufflé dish. Bake in the middle of the oven for about 45 to 60 minutes, or until the soufflé has risen and turned a lovely light brown. Serve immediately.

PASTA AL FORNO BAKED PASTA serves 8 to 12

This is a famous and traditional dish in Italy, particularly in and around Palermo in Sicily. It is a dish used for festive occasions when families gather, Christmas being one of the most important. It makes a wonderful dish for a very large party, especially a buffet, because it is plentiful and easy to serve. For me, this dish has much the same effect as madeleines did for Marcel Proust. Boyhood memories leap forth when I eat Pasta al Forno, which was always made with such love by my family. SUGGESTED WINES: CHIANTI CLASSICO OR NERO D'AVOLA

NOTE: Any leftover sauce will store well in the refrigerator for up to 5 days; it can also be frozen for some time.

10 cups (plus a little extra) Salsa di Pomodoro Stracotto (Slow Tomato Sauce, page 18 and method at right)

2 pounds beef rump or pork butt roast

1/2 cup dried unflavored bread crumbs

1 1/2 pounds best-quality large or small dried pasta, such as spaghetti, rotelle, mostaccioli, or rigatoni

4 hard-boiled eggs, sliced 1/4 inch thick

1 cup fresh or frozen tiny peas (thawed)

To make the meat sauce, prepare the tomato sauce as directed in the recipe, adding the meat in one solid piece. Cook slowly for up to 3 hours.

Prepare a 4-quart ovenproof casserole by spreading a moderate amount of butter on its sides and bottom. Pour in 1/4 cup of the bread crumbs and twist and turn the casserole until the sides and bottom are evenly coated with crumbs. Gently shake out any excess. Set aside.

Remove the piece of meat from the sauce and let it cool to room temperature. Shred it with a fork. (Do not cut it if possible.) Transfer to a bowl and set aside.

¾ **cup freshly grated Romano or Parmesan cheese**

Sea salt and freshly ground black pepper

Cook the pasta very al dente (see page 13), and drain well. Return the pasta to the cooking pot and toss it with a very small amount of the tomato sauce.

Preheat the oven to 350°F. To assemble the casserole in the prepared baking dish, place a generous layer of pasta, a generous layer of shredded meat, some egg slices, some peas, some grated cheese, and some sauce, and sprinkle on a little salt and pepper. Repeat, finishing with a layer of pasta. Sprinkle the top with cheese, the remaining ¼ cup bread crumbs, and a little more sauce.

Bake for about 1½ hours. When the top and sides are golden brown, remove from the oven and let it rest 20 minutes before serving. It may also be turned out onto a plate or a cutting board and sliced as you would a cake. Extra sauce may be served with the slices, though it is neither necessary nor traditional.

VERMICELLI AL FORNO ULTRATHIN PASTA, BAKED

serves 6

My own family has grown very fond of this dish served as a delicate first-course pasta. We do it *sformato,* turned out of individual ovenproof ramekins onto a light tomato sauce covering the center of a small plate. It makes a decorative and tasty starter for an important meal. With the distinctive taste of the slightly bitter black olives, it is particularly good before an entrée with a strong flavor, such as roasted or braised fowl or game. SUGGESTED WINES: CHARDONNAY OR PINOT GRIGIO

8 black Sicilian or kalamata olives, pitted and coarsely chopped

4 slices prosciutto di Parma, finely chopped

A few large capers, chopped

3 to 4 tablespoons dried unflavored bread crumbs

1/3 cup chopped fresh Italian parsley

4 teaspoons extra virgin olive oil, plus a little for the pasta

Sea salt and freshly ground black pepper

10 ounces dried vermicelli

Generously butter a 2-quart ovenproof casserole, or individual ovenproof dishes that will just hold all the ingredients. Set aside. Preheat the oven to 400°F.

To make the "sauce," put the olives, prosciutto, capers, bread crumbs, parsley, the 4 teaspoons oil, and salt and pepper into a large, heavy skillet and cook gently over low heat until everything is just heated through to blend the flavors. Set aside.

Meanwhile, cook the pasta al dente (see page 13). (Watch the cooking carefully, because this pasta is thin and cooks very quickly.) Drain the pasta well, return it to the cooking pot, and toss it in a little oil to keep it from sticking together. Add the "sauce" and mix thoroughly. Put the mixture into the prepared casserole or

2 large eggs, beaten

1/3 cup freshly grated Parmesan cheese, for sprinkling

1 cup Salsa al Pomodoro (Quick Tomato Sauce, page 19), plus 1 or 2 spoonfuls of heavy cream (optional)

individual dishes. Pour the beaten eggs over the pasta and sprinkle on the cheese.

Bake for 20 to 25 minutes, or until a lovely golden crust is formed on the top and, with luck, also on the sides. Remove from the oven and allow to rest for a few minutes. Combine the tomato sauce and cream, spoon the mixture onto a serving platter, and turn out the pasta onto the sauce. If the pasta is well set, you could turn it out onto a plate and cut into wedges as you would cut a pie. Serve.

PASTA E FAGIOLI PASTA AND BEANS serves 8

This dish is famous as "pasta fazool," and can be made in many ways. Again, this is practically a vegetarian dish—just omit the ham—and a hearty one, particularly suited to cold weather. Be sure to set the beans to soak the night before you plan to make this soup. SUGGESTED WINE: GRECO DI TUFO OR PINOT NOIR

2 cups dried white cannellini or great Northern beans, soaked overnight in cold water

1 ounce prosciutto di Parma, including skin, or lean salt pork

1 large yellow onion, cut into medium dice

2 garlic cloves, well crushed

¼ cup extra virgin olive oil

Sea salt

¼ teaspoon freshly ground black pepper

8 ounces dried small, short macaroni

¼ cup freshly grated Parmesan cheese, for passing

Drain the beans, then place them and the prosciutto, onion, garlic, olive oil, salt, and pepper in a small stockpot. Add enough water to cover. Bring to a simmer over medium heat and cook gently until the beans are soft, but not mushy, 30 to 40 minutes.

Have heated serving bowls ready. If all of the water is absorbed, add more boiling water or some stock. Add the pasta and cook until it is just done, al dente, not mushy, about 8 minutes. (Remember that the pasta will absorb some of the liquid, unless you cook it separately in plain water.) The soup should be quite dense.

Serve it hot in the heated bowls and pass the cheese as well as the pepper mill at the table.

VARIATION: For a Tuscan version of this soup, add a generous cup of coarsely chopped fresh or canned tomatoes. For a Venetian version, use red kidney beans instead of the white, and add a healthy pinch of cinnamon.

INDEX